PROVOKING SUPERNATURAL UPRGRADE

MOVING FROM RUINS TO RULE

LESTO
editora
2019

ISAAC MAXWELL NWANJI

Copyright © 2019 by Isaac Maxwell Nwanji.

Cover design   Isaac Maxwell Nwanji
Graphic design Lesto Editora

Editorial   Áthila Pereira Pelá
                Jordana Domingues

Dados Internacionais de Catalogação na Publicação (CIP)
Angélica Ilacqua CRB-8/7057

Nwanji, Isaac Maxwell
    Provoking supernatural upgrade : moving from ruins to rule / Isaac Maxwell Nwanji. –- São Paulo : Lesto, 2019.

240 p.

ISBN: 978-65-80458-06-6

1. Cristianismo 2. Deus 3. Palavra de Deus I. Título

19-1468   CDD 230

Índices para catálogo sistemático:
1. Religião : Cristianismo

Printed in Brazil

All rights reserved.

Dedication

First and foremost, praise and thanks goes to my Lord Jesus Christ for enabling grace, and for the many blessings undeservingly bestowed upon my life. This book is to your honor my King!

I also dedicate this book to my precious wife, Fortune and my three beautiful daughters Kamsi, Munachi and Dalu for their profound love and warm encouragement. And also, for their ever-inspiring support, prayers, timely counsel and strategic insights to ensuring that this book and many other projects became a reality. I also dedicate this book to the dynamic Citizens of PECULIAR NATION IN CHRIST. I am very proud of you and your uncompromising peculiar resolve that there is no higher miracle anywhere than a life transformed by the word of God.

Finally, to my family and the great men and women of God who were used by God to nurture me. They have all been an incalculable and boundless blessing to my life over the years, contributing to my spiritual and mental makeup in life and in ministry. Honor and appreciations beyond words!

CONTENT

Introduction 7

Chapter 1
The Chosen David And The Chosen Stewards 10

Chapter 2
Corresponding Factors Of Influence 30

Chapter 3
From Within To Without 46

Chapter 4
From Isolation To Recommendation 59

Chapter 5
Full Of The Holy Spirit 68

Chapter 6
Divine Wisdom - Prudent In Matters 76

Chapter 7
Responsible Service 89

Chapter 8
Experiencing Supernatural Upgrade 99

Chapter 9
Joseph – The Man Who Moved
From Ruins To Rule! 142

Chapter 10
The Rough And Bumpy Ride – The Process! 178

Chapter 11
Recorgnising God's Plan – Walking In It! 196

Chapter 12
All Round Transformation 222

Conclusion 234

Introduction

For which of you, intending to build a tower, sitteth not down first, and counteth the cost, whether he have sufficient to finish it? Lest haply, after he hath laid the foundation, and is not able to finish it, all that behold it begin to mock him, Saying, This man began to build, and was not able to finish. **Luke 14: 28-30(KJV)**

This scripture is contextually precise on the need for planning and determining the cost of achievement in life. Everyone wants to achieve but no one is ready to perceive. The sincere truth is that no achievement is possible without considering or determining the cost of achievement.

If you desire to build a new mansion, and you don't sit down to figure the cost of building in order to determine whether or not you have what it takes to finish it, then what you would have at the end of the day is an abandoned project – an uncompleted building. You would run out of money and required resources.

You become an object of mockery to passersby as the unwise man who desired great achievement but lacked what it took to deliver.

To desire a thing is not enough. Cost determination is key as far as achievement is concerned!

Therefore, in the light of the scripture above, it is clear that you cannot construct building blocks where there is no lower grounded base (foundation). Also, you cannot add a roof where there are no constructed roofing blocks. This is the standard procedure for building, and this must be followed by any builder, otherwise collapse is inevitable!

No one in history ever achieved greatness or attained a position of eternal value starting from the top. They began building from the bottom, and gradually raised the building, upgrading it to the top. This exactly is the laid down pattern of life. This is the design given to existence by the Master of the universe. The only thing that begins from the top and ends at the bottom is the grave!

Favor goes not where grace is absent. But if we are sincere, humble and careful enough to identify and follow the Master's pattern, then it becomes impossible for us to be battered by the unfavorable events of life!

I invite you to follow me carefully through this Spirit empowered blueprint for effective actualization of destiny and purpose – navigating out of the ruins of the troubles and the misfortunes of life, to the place of dominion and authority in Christ Jesus!

PRAYER LINE!

May the anointing and wisdom to finish well, and to finish strong in all my endeavors be released upon me right now. In the name of Jesus, Amen!

Chapter 1

The chosen David and the Seven Stewards

Let us carefully observe a scriptural juxtaposition between the chosen David and the seven men that were chosen to serve tables. Seeing the connecting similarity between these two phenomenal parties should excite our spirits. David and the seven chosen stewards existed on the earth but lived in two different generations. On the historical timeline, they both existed at two points extensive apart, two extensively distant points on the historical timeline. A time believed by bible scholars to be approximately 1500 years apart.

Yet we see such outstanding similarities between these two. We see such profound connections – drawn together by similar virtues, merits, attributes, and characteristics. A grand similarity enabled by same Spirit, of course!

To achieve this, **there is need for a systematic comparison of these two key scriptures:**

1 Samuel 16: 14-19 (KJV)

14. *But the Spirit of the Lord departed from Saul, and an evil spirit from the Lord troubled him.*

15. *And Saul's servants said unto him, Behold now, an evil spirit from God troubleth thee.*

16. *Let our lord now command thy servants, which are before thee, to seek out a man, who is a cunning player on an harp: and it shall come to pass, when the evil spirit from God is upon thee, that he shall play with his hand, and thou shalt be well.*

17. *And Saul said unto his servants, Provide me now a man that can play well, and bring him to me.*

18. *Then answered one of the servants, and said, Behold, I have seen a son of Jesse the Bethlehemite, that is cunning in playing, and a mighty valiant man, and a man of war, and prudent in matters, and a comely person, and the Lord is with him.*

19. *Wherefore Saul sent messengers unto Jesse, and said, Send me David thy son, which is with the sheep.*

And

Acts 6:1-8 (KJV)

1. *And in those days, when the number of the disciples was multiplied, there arose a murmuring of the Grecians against the Hebrews, because their widows were neglected in the daily ministration.*

2. Then the twelve called the multitude of the disciples unto them, and said, It is not reason that we should leave the word of God, and serve tables.
3. Wherefore, brethren, look ye out among you seven men of honest report, full of the Holy Ghost and wisdom, whom we may appoint over this business.
4. But we will give ourselves continually to prayer, and to the ministry of the word.
5. And the saying pleased the whole multitude: and they chose Stephen, a man full of faith and of the Holy Ghost, and Philip, and Prochorus, and Nicanor, and Timon, and Parmenas, and Nicolas a proselyte of Antioch:
6. Whom they set before the apostles: and when they had prayed, they laid their hands on them.
7. And the word of God increased; and the number of the disciples multiplied in Jerusalem greatly; and a great company of the priests were obedient to the faith.
8. And Stephen, full of faith and power, did great wonders and miracles among the people.

Together, let us ponder the Father's intent through the Holy Scriptures, comparing and harmonizing the insights and wisdom embedded in these two distinct and distant point in biblical timeline. These are indeed unparalleled examples of eternal reference to true conquests in the Kingdom.

I very strongly believe that destiny and purpose are unveiled by engaging the "Word" through careful reflection and deep considerations; by uniting ourselves through the power of the Spirit to the daily revelations unveiled to us in the word. When we yield our everyday life to the demands of God's word, completely harmonizing our daily thoughts, perceptions, inclinations and actions to the revealed truth in the word of God, most assuredly, defeat and failure will be kept at bay. **We cannot be positioned by the word of God, piloted by the Spirit of Grace, and not exercise dominion over the issues of life!**

PRAYER LINE!

Dear Father, this day I commit to the daily study and application of Your word in my life. I receive grace to harmonize my thoughts and actions with Your word. Let the promises of Your word be made manifest in my life. By Your word let my life be honored. Amen!

The lines of **1Samuel 16: 14-19** sighted above speak of a moment in time when the Spirit of the Lord departed from Saul on account of his disobedience to the word of God. Before we proceed further, let's take a moment to understand the background upon which Saul, the first King of Israel was rejected of the Lord.

Unlike what was obtainable in neighboring nations, kingship in Israel was supposed to be under the direct leadership or directorate of the God of Israel. While the King of neighboring nations exercised full dictatorship dominance over his subjects, Israel's king was not to considered himself as final authority. The kings of Israel were under the law of Moses, issued by the scribes.

Pretty much like every other citizen of the nation of Israel were under the constituted authority of the Mosaic Law, so was also the king of Israel.

Seeing that Saul was the first king of Israel, the example that Saul set, being the first of Israel's kings, would definitely influence, positively or negatively, all succeeding kings. It's no wonder he was held to stringent standard. But Saul erred, and made trivial the standards set for him.

Firstly, at a time when Saul moved against the Philistines in battle, he waited eagerly for Samuel the priest to come and offer sacrifices to seek God's favor. But as Samuel delayed in coming, Saul offered the sacrifices himself, **1 Samuel 13: 9**. The offering of sacrifices was a religious duty delegated to the priest by the Law. But Saul, running out of patience with Samuel, arrogantly offered the sacrifice himself, assuming the rights of a priest. When Samuel eventually arrived, he told Saul:

> "...Thou hast done foolishly: thou hast not kept the commandment of the Lord thy God, which he commanded thee: for now, would the Lord have established thy kingdom upon Israel forever. But now thy kingdom shall not continue: The Lord hath sought him a man after his own heart, and the Lord hath commanded him to be captain over his people, because thou hast not kept that which the Lord commanded thee." **1 Samuel 13:13-14 (KJV).**

Samuel pronounced an end to Saul's kingdom. This implied that Saul's family would not create a reign. Saul would lose the throne to a different family.

Also, in another instant, God commanded Saul to totally destroy the Amalekites together with everything they had. Saul was to be an agent of divine judgement against Amalek for resisting Israel when they proceeded from Egypt. But we read that:

> "...Saul and the people spared Agag, and the best of the sheep, and of the oxen, and of the fatlings, and the lambs, and all that was good, and would not utterly destroy them..." **1Samuel 15: 9 (KJV).**

Saul carried out this invasion as if it were a common war that he was leading. He ordered his preferences, and disdained the commandment of God. Saul misrepresented the character of divine judgment. Once again, he abused the privilege giving him as the first of Israel's king.

And to this sacrilegious conduct, Samuel's pronouncement, among many others, upon Saul was this:

> *"For rebellion is as the sin of witchcraft, and stubbornness is as iniquity and idolatry. Because thou hast rejected the word of the Lord, he hath also rejected thee from being king"* **1Samuel 15:23 (KJV).**

What follows is a directive from God to Samuel, ordering him to the house of Jesse, to anoint his son David. And Samuel, upon anointing David, the Spirit of the Lord came upon David, but consequently,

> *"...the Spirit of the Lord departed from Saul, and an evil spirit from the Lord troubled him"* **1Samuel 16:14 (KJV).**

The very instant the Spirit of God left Saul, an evil spirit came upon him. Saul was terrified as a result, because it's not a pleasant experience for the spirit of God to depart from any man! This experience made Saul's advisors to recommend a solution to his predicament of terrible mental condition that drove him mad. They needed someone whose playing of the harp would relieve the king of his trauma and dementia. **In desperation** for some solution, one of the king's advisers offered his recommendation;

> "...Behold, I have seen a son of Jesse the Bethlehemite, that is cunning in playing, and a mighty valiant man, and a man of war, and prudent in matters, and a comely person, and the Lord is with him" **1Samuel 16:18 (KJV)**.

Highlighting the credentials that distinguished this young son of Jesse, it isn't hard to see that he had been prepared for this moment of honor. God had prepared him for this encounter with destiny. It is amusing to see how men hope for great encounters in their life, but remain unprepared for it. Just like we see in the case of the son of Jesse, unusual destiny encounters are tactically delivered to us by the operations of God's work of wisdom. They are delivered to us in God's own way, and at His own timing. However, most importantly, they are delivered to us only when we are found to be prepared for it. God delivers nothing **to** the hands of unprepared men!

Now, considering the credentials of this young man, we see firstly that he was *"...cunning in playing..."*, he was very skillful in the playing of his music instrument. Not only did he play it, he played it well. He played so well that his ability was both recognized and acknowledged. In respect to the playing of his harp, he was a man of **EXCELLENCE**.

Secondly, this young son of Jesse was accounted to be *"...a mighty valiant man..."* and *"...a mighty man of war..."* He was known for his great courage. His heroic abilities were well known. He alone kept the flocks of Jesse his father. The strength of courage and sense of confidence with which he followed after the things of life put him in a class of mighty warriors. It is believed that sometimes he remained in the fields for days by himself keeping watch over the sheepfold, and resisting the lions and the bears which made attempt to prey on the sheep. David was a man of **COURAGE**.

Thirdly, young David was a man known to be *"...prudent in matters..."* His good sense of judgement was known of many. The discretion with which he followed after the demands of duty earned him a recognition. Young David must have proven himself to be of good prudence seeing Jesse his father was confident to leave the family's sheepfold at his hands alone. Indeed, he was known to be of **PRUDENCE**.

Fourthly, a featured peculiarity of young David from the text reference, is that he was *"...a comely person..."* He was good looking, graceful and quite a pleasant young man. We cannot dispute the fact that young David did take good care of himself. He was well groomed. He paid keen attention to his personal appearance. Though a shepherd boy, nonetheless, he took good care of himself. David was a man with **PLEASANT APPEARANCE.**

And fifthly, concerning young David, it is reported that *"...the Lord is with him..."* No one could doubt that God was with David. He carried the presence of God. God's favor was seen in his life. The Hand of God was evidently upon him. His playing skill, his courageous heart, his good sense of judgement, his graceful appearance could only have indications of God's Hand upon his life. It could only have been by the Hand of God that young David was able to slay a lion and a bear with his bare hands, **1Samuel 17: 34-36**. Indeed, David carried **THE PRESENCE OF GOD.**

Now, when Saul heard of all these merits possessed by just one man, he immediately sent messengers to Jesse, requesting the presence of his son David. Who wouldn't want to be honored by the presence of anyone with these estimable credentials?

Saul wasted no time requesting the presence of young David knowing that there weren't **many** in Israel that have proven themselves to be of this much value.

Let's again highlight the features of David's merits – those attributes that earned him a spot in the palace, a place in the king's life, and a home in the king's family:

- EXCELLENCE
- COURAGE
- PRUDENCE
- PLEASANT APPEARANCE
- THE PRESENCE OF GOD

It is not possible to have such attributes as these and not be a man after God's heart! These qualities have tremendous capacity to draw men to you. These qualities are what places value in a man's life. Anyone having these qualities, as David did, is ready for an encounter with destiny. These are the merits that brings a man before the kings of the earth. These are the attributes in a man's life that places demand for his presence. These here are the things that makes for greatness.

PRAYER LINE!

My Father, grant me what it takes to be singled out for opportunities. I receive grace to manifest attributes that will make my generation reckon with me. Father, put my name in the hearts and lips of men – in my favor, and to my honor, let them make mention of me. Amen!

On the other hand, we see that right after the ascension of our Lord Jesus Christ, **followed the descent of the promised Holy Spirit on the day of Pentecost.** On this glorious Pentecost day were the believers baptized into one body, the church. Right after the baptism of the Holy Spirit, an alarming rate of church growth was recorded.

Now, during this time, as the disciples were increasing in numbers by leaps and bounds, <u>ill feelings</u> developed among the Greek-speaking believers known as "Hellenists" towards the Hebrew-speaking believers because their widows were being discriminated against in the daily food lines. The Twelve apostles therefore called a meeting of the disciples. And it was explained that it was somewhat inappropriate and imprudent to set the daily welfare distributions in priority over the discipline of the word. They explained that it was indiscreet of them being apostles to commit themselves to the supervision of the daily welfare ministrations, at the expense of the greater responsibility of preaching and teaching God's word.

Therefore, unanimously all agreed to the decision to choose seven men from among them whom they all trusted to be of good reputation, and also to be full of the Holy Spirit, and having good sense of judgement. These chosen men were assigned for task performance of service.

Apparently, this came forward as a brilliant idea to all. The congregation thought this was a great remedy. Thus, the following men were chosen for this ministry:

- STEPHEN
- PHILIP
- PROCHORUS
- NICANOR
- TIMON
- PARMENAS
- NICOLAS

Having chosen these men, they were presented to the apostles. And in prayers, the apostles laid hands on them, and commissioned them for their task. Consequently, peace was restored, minds were healed of resentments, and the church flourished. As a result of this division of kingdom labor, the Word of God prospered. The number of disciples in Jerusalem increased dramatically, and a great number of priests submitted themselves to the faith.

As seen in the scripture above, the criteria that formed the basis for the admission of these men into the stewardship are vivid enough. Please let's take note of the following attributes that qualified the seven to be chosen.

The emphases are seen in the 3rd verse of the chapter.

> "Wherefore, brethren, look ye out among you seven men of honest report, full of the Holy Ghost and wisdom, whom we may appoint over this business." **Acts 6: 3 (KJV)**

Some may be wondering why the emphasis on seven men. Some also have suggested that the decision for seven men was based on the fact that the number seven was considered a sacred number among the Hebrews. Though there isn't particularly any reason to suggest that the apostle's choice for seven had anything to do with the religious significance associated with the number seven.

I choose to believe the decision for choosing seven men was based on the fact that it may have been a suitable number, adequate enough to meet the demands of the assignment.

Now, these men were to be *"...of honest report..."* by implication, they were to be of good reputation. They were those regarded not by the religious circle alone, but by the general public as men of integrity. They were men of whom the public gave good testimony; well-known and accredited. <u>**They were men whose character were well known and just.**</u> They were men of **GOOD REPUTATION**.

Secondly, these men must be men known to be *"...full of the Holy Ghost..."* by implication, they must be men known to be endowed of the Lord. They must be men whose lives are particularly recognized to be under the <u>**control**</u> of the Holy Spirit. Not only were they men saved by the grace of Christ, and made partakers of the Holy Spirit, but they were men whose lives demonstrated the presence of God. They were men whose lives were **FULL OF THE HOLY SPIRIT**.

Thirdly, these men were also to be men of *"...wisdom..."*, meaning that they had to be men of prudence and far-sightedness. These seven men had to be men well known for their good discretion. Men whose lifestyle gave evidence to their insight, knowledge and good understanding. They were men known to revere God and upright in their daily enterprise. They were men known to be impartial and broadminded in judgment. They were men **FULL OF WISDOM.**

And fourthly, these men must be those whose appointment "...*over this business*..." could be trusted. They must be men reckoned with due diligence to duties and responsibilities. They must be men known to serve; men known to give their time, energy and resources to the **furtherance of the objectives for which they represent.** These seven men must be men acknowledged for their stern commitment and unbroken faithfulness in their pursuit of the goals set before them. They were men known to resent failure, men who do not accept defeat. These seven were men of **SERVICE!**

From the forgoing therefore, we reason that the underlying distinctive feature that qualified these seven men are thus:

- GOOD REPUTATION
- FULL OF THE SPIRIT
- WISDOM
- SERVICE

Now, note this very carefully, these attributes are what it takes for any man or woman to achieve kingdom excellence, success, advancement and prosperity. In a world of increasing insecurity, depravity and agitation these attributes must be well rooted in the life of anyone who will command a meaningful life, and make sustainable impart towards kingdom advancement. It is true that God can use anyone regardless of notable character flaws and deficiency, however, any life found to be embellished with these qualities

> *"...shall be a vessel unto honour, sanctified, and meet for the master's use, and prepared unto every good work"* **2Timothy 2: 21 (KJV)**.

Any man, having a life garnished with these qualities or attributes would always standout among others. Anyone in whose life these admirable virtues are well engrained will ever be a candidate of consideration for all honorable appointments. These qualities will always put a man above his contemporaries. These qualities aforementioned are what places value in a man's life. These are the merits that distinguishes any man, and puts him in a class by himself. Here they are again:

- GOOD REPUTATION
- FULL OF THE SPIRIT
- WISDOM
- SERVICE

Permit me to note this; no one will go far with God in whose life these merits are not found. No lasting relationship is elusive of these qualities. Even the world, as dark and wicked as it is, are in desperate search of men whom can be trusted, men who have distinguished themselves with these attributes. On every preference scale, men of such repute will always come before and ahead of others, as it was with the seven whom were chosen for the stewardship.

These attributes are excellent leadership qualities with the dynamic capacity to effect change, growth and development in any organization, or nation. The most disconcerting challenge confronting the nations of the world today as we see it is the scarcity of leaders in whom these aforementioned merits abide. Excellent leadership delivery is ever upon the patronage of these qualities. Every organization that will make meaningful progression will be one that thrives under the leadership of these merits.

PRAYER LINE!

Right now, I receive capacity to standout. I receive what it takes to be chosen amongst my peers in this generation. I declare that where others encounter disappointment, I encounter divine appointments. I declare that I receive what it takes to be productive and resourceful in all endeavor. Amen!

Now, let's begin to lay in an orderly fashion a comparison of these two separate personalities, David the son of Jesse, and the Seven Stewards of the early church. Though these two appear to be in somewhat similar class they are indeed separated by a considerable length of time on the biblical timeline. A close examination of these two reveal the connectivity of dispositions and the **underlying** features that positions men for extraordinary encounters in destiny.

◩ PROPHETIC INTERJECTION

In the name of Jesus, I pray, my Father, may Your Heavens invade the earth on my behalf today to position me for a season of supernatural advantage on all fronts of endeavor, in Jesus mighty name, Amen!!!

"Until the spirit be poured upon us from on high, and the wilderness be a fruitful field, and the fruitful field be counted for a forest" **Isaiah 32: 15 (KJV).**

King of Glory, may I be positioned from this moment for an outpouring of the Spirit that will interrupt the unending habitation of the spirit of barrenness and impotence over the affairs of my life, in Jesus' name. Lord, let the motions and the stronghold of the wilderness places of my life, be overthrown for a fruitful field, In Jesus' name, Amen!

Chapter 2

Corresponding Factors of Influence

Certain common factors come to great light when we take into consideration the similarity in the background that featured the emergence of David the young son of Jesse, and the advent of the Seven Stewards of the early church. The similarities that play out in these two events of scripture brings out very helpful kingdom principles that may be applied to our advantage.

FIRST COMMON FACTOR

A peculiarity found with both sceneries is that there was first a necessity. There was a basic need – an essential requirement.

We read concerning the background that necessitated the demand for the son of Jesse:

> "Let our lord now command thy servants, which are before thee, to seek out a man, who

is a cunning player on an harp: and it shall come to pass, when the evil spirit from God is upon thee, that he shall play with his hand, and thou shalt be well." **1 Samuel 16: 16 (KJV)**

Under the horrible pain of madness inflicted by the evil spirit, Saul was desperate for healing. He would give just about anything to be relieved of these torments. He needed help, and he needed it desperately. Saul's desperate need for solution necessitated the emergence of David. The circumstances surrounding Saul's life created an obligation that was inevitable as far as Saul was concerned. Saul was distressed. He was in frantic need. His servants were anxious to see their king restored. As far as the king was in **distress** all around him were in unrest. Everyone looked to see the king restored to health – there was a need!

Looking again at the background that necessitated the demand for the seven stewards in the early church of Christ, we read thus:

Acts 6: 1-3 (KJV)

1. *And in those days, when the number of the disciples was multiplied, there arose a murmuring of the Grecians against the Hebrews, because their widows were neglected in the daily ministration.*

2. *Then the twelve called the multitude of the disciples unto them, and said, It is not reason that we should leave the word of God, and serve tables.*

3. *Wherefore, brethren, look ye out among you seven men of honest report, full of the Holy Ghost and wisdom, whom we may appoint over this business.*

We see from the above text that an occasion had occurred that necessitated the need for the appointment of stewards. When the body of believers were yet in rather small number, the charities were conveniently distributed by the hands of the apostles. Thus, we read that many disciples in the earliest church in the spirit of benevolence, sold off their properties, and,

> "*...brought the prices of the things that were sold, And laid them down at the apostles' feet: and distribution was made unto every man according as he had need*" **Acts 4: 34-35 (KJV).**

But as the church was greatly increased, so also did the daily collections. Seeing that the contributions increased, and it was now increasingly difficult for the apostles to manage an even distribution of the donations without being distracted by it, it became imperatively necessary that this matter should be entrusted to the responsibility of certain men, the Hebrews.

But amongst the disciples were the Grecians. These were Jews who were scattered among the Gentiles. They spoke the Greek language, and used the Greek translation of the Old Testament, called the Septuagint in their synagogues. The Grecians were also called the Hellenists. And these Grecians at that time began to murmur against the Hebrews, for their partiality in the daily charity. The Grecians claimed their widows were cheated. This despondency expressed by the Grecians in the church **necessitated** the need for not just stewards, but stewards with qualified credentials.

In both backgrounds, we see the compelling circumstances that created the need for the services of David and the seven stewards respectively. In both backgrounds, we see how the unfolding situations obligated the demand for the presence of David and the seven stewards respectively. The condition of the moment left no room for alternative – the people simply could not have done otherwise. They were left with no choice but to satisfy the somewhat overbearing need at hand.

Take a look around you, everywhere, every time and every day, there are lots of situations placing demands for your value. There are circumstances requiring your services. There are lots of empty spaces to be occupied and vacuum to fill but many of us cannot see them.

We simply cannot see them because most of the time we are looking in the wrong places. There are needs that require our attention.

There are voids calling for our fill. There are situations awaiting our manifestation. Life is really not meaningful if we are yet to find that thing we give value to. Like David we are all instruments of healing to a degenerated world. And like the seven stewards we are all vessels of peace, solace and stability. Life is truly about living for the health of something. Until we have found that for which we truly live, we are merely existing – not living!

But the thing is this, we keep seeking for the wrong places. We seek for where we may be accepted, where we may be accommodated, but not where we are truly needed. Rather than seeking for that place where our presence will add value, we often settle for where our needs are satisfied. Well, as great as the satisfaction of our needs may sound, we must understand that no one ever made significant impart in life by simply living only for the satisfaction of personal needs. Life is much more than such narrow mindedness.

Until we begin to make a difference, we are yet to experience the joy and beauty of life. Honor is never bestowed upon the platform of irrelevance. Honor comes only to those who have proven relevant, important, valuable, useful, helpful, constructive and indispensable. Let us muster the courage to 'step up' and 'step out' to those places our values are truly confirmed. Beloved, believe this, you have what it takes to make a difference. And making a difference is what gives value to a life. Let's make the desired difference in those places that need a difference. Irrespective of how seemingly insignificant the difference may be, it is nonetheless a difference.

The greatest imparts in life begin with an easy and simply, yet confident step. It matters not how inconsequential the difference may be, there is nothing more rewarding than the joy of knowing you just made a difference. Simply offering a glass of water to satisfy the thirsty is pretty much an impart as facilitating a successful peaceful resolution between two conflicting nations. Let's make a difference – let's make an impact!

You need to say to yourself, "I am determined to flow in the frequency of David the son of Jesse and the Seven Stewards, and I must start filling up those voids that demand my input.

PRAYER LINE!

Lord, open my eyes to see what you have designed for me - that I may be fulfilled in life and ministry. Open my eyes to see those places calling for my help. Open my eyes to see the difference I can make in my generation. Father, may I not live a life of no-impart. Amen!

SECOND COMMON FACTOR

A second peculiarity found with both sceneries is that there was as an agency of recommendation. Yes, they were recommended for the assignment, but most importantly they were recommended by an intermediary party. Someone confirmed them as being worthy of the task. Someone attested of their credentials, and their ability to deliver on the mandate. Someone endorsed them!

Again, we read in respect of Saul's dementia:

1 Samuel 16: 15-17 (KJV)

15. *And Saul's servants said unto him, Behold now, an evil spirit from God troubleth thee.*

16. *Let our lord now command thy servants, which are before thee, to seek out a man, who is a cunning player on an harp: and it shall come to pass, when the evil spirit from God is upon thee, that he shall play with his hand, and thou shalt be well.*

17. *And Saul said unto his servants, Provide me now a man that can play well, and bring him to me.*

We read from the above that a suggestion was proffered by Saul's servant in respect to his affliction. And Saul, having acknowledged the counsel of his servant demanded the presence of *"…a man that can play well…"* to be brought before him. Now, look well to the response of a servant of his:

> *"Then answered one of the servants, and said, Behold, I have seen a son of Jesse the Bethlehemite, that is cunning in playing, and a mighty valiant man, and a man of war, and prudent in matters, and a comely person, and the Lord is with him"* **1Samuel 16: 18 (KJV)**.

Read again; *"Then answered one of the servants, and said, Behold, I have seen a son of Jesse the Bethlehemite…"* It is rather interesting that this particular servant of Saul isn't identified by a name, yet he played about the most significant role in David's encounter with destiny. This unnamed servant of Saul was the key to the rise of David.

This servant was the connecting point between the son of Jesse and the King. Had he held his peace and refrained himself from speaking, perhaps David may never had seen the throne whereupon he would afterward sit as the King of Israel. This servant of Saul was the voice of recommendation God had raised at that moment to speak in favor of David. He was the bridge for David. David was recommended for the task.

Another examination of the circumstances surrounding the early church reveals similar factor. We read:

Acts 6: 3-5 (KJV)

3. *Wherefore, brethren, look ye out among you seven men of honest report, full of the Holy Ghost and wisdom, whom we may appoint over this business.*

4. *But we will give ourselves continually to prayer, and to the ministry of the word.*

5. *And the saying pleased the whole multitude: and they chose Stephen, a man full of faith and of the Holy Ghost, and Philip, and Prochorus, and Nicanor, and Timon, and Parmenas, and Nicolas a proselyte of Antioch.*

Similarly, we see from the above that a suggestion was proffered this time by the apostles, and the church acknowledged it;

"...And the saying pleased the whole multitude..." **v5**.

We also read that the multitudes, *"...chose Stephen, a man full of faith and of the Holy Ghost, and Philip, and Prochorus, and Nicanor, and Timon, and Parmenas, and Nicolas a proselyte of Antioch"* **v5**.

The Seven Stewards were chosen. They were chosen on the basis of the favorable recommendations from individual persons. Apparently, some persons endorsed them for the task. Certain persons must have put forward the credentials of these seven men. They were chosen because they were recommended for the task.

Beloved, recommendation remains key to supernatural elevation in life. Someone must necessarily speak in favor of you.

For the office you desire, one must necessarily recommend you. For the business you pursue, one must necessarily endorse you. You may be the best at what you do, but being best is not enough to get you scaling the heights of life. Had the butler not made mention of Joseph before Pharaoh we cannot tell what may have become of Joseph.

The Lord Jesus Christ received the Spirit without measure, and being the Son of God, **it was within His rights to use His Father's authority to His advantage.** Nonetheless, we see that the Lord followed the Kingdom order of things. We see that it was necessary to have John **the** Baptist point Him to the people **with these words,**

"...*Behold the Lamb of God, which taketh away the sin of the world*" **John 1: 29 (KJV).**

My prayer for you is that God will raise voices of recommendation in your favor in every time of your need.

My prayer for you is that those who must speak in your favor will lose their peace until they open their mouth and begin to speak forth the good things concerning you.

My prayer for you is that God will position men and women who will point you to the world – men and women who will announce you and blow your trumpet, Amen!

PRAYER LINE!

Father place men and women in positions to speak in my favor. Raise voices of recommendation concerning every area of my life. Compel those whom you have positioned for me to open their mouth and speak forth. Amen!

THIRD COMMON FACTOR

A third peculiarity found with both sceneries is that not only were the son of Jesse and the Seven Stewards recommended, but their recommendation came on account of their credentials. They were endorsed on account of proof of ability and trustworthiness. The recommendations of these men came not **necessarily** by favoritism or personal sentiments but by their abilities and attributes, by which they **have** been certified by the general public to **their credit.** They were chosen based on the qualities that distinguished them.

The credentials for which David was chosen is very clear:

> "Then answered one of the servants, and said, Behold, I have seen a son of Jesse the Bethlehemite, that is cunning in playing, and a mighty valiant man, and a man of war, and prudent in matters, and a comely person, and the Lord is with him" **1Samuel 16: 18 (KJV).**

I do not think that David was the only young man in Israel who played excellently on the harp. But it is agreeable that a brilliant hand on the harp was not all that was required for the task here. More than just playing well on a musical instrument was required here. And it seemed young David had it all in one. Added to his playing skills, he was a brave young man with a warrior's heart. He was known for his honesty and good discretion. Oh! he was also well groomed and had a pleasant appearance. And most importantly, the Hand of God was evident in his life.

And let me dwell on young David's comeliness a little bit. Grooming and personal appearance is something **many trivialize today.** Some in the church have wrongly associated the need to admirable and pleasant appearance with carnality and worldliness.

Oh no, this is so very wrong! As a matter of fact, good grooming is as much a spiritual discipline as praying and fasting.

There is absolutely nothing in scripture that promotes poor grooming or poor hygiene. Nothing in scripture endorses an unpleasant presence. It makes no sense offending the **sensibilities** of those from whom you hope to have favor. I mean, everyone appreciates the presence of pleasant things, including a pleasant appearance. People have lost great opportunities simply because their presence offended the impression of those they stood before. Let's be wise!

Again, we read of the endorsement of the seven Stewards:

> "*Wherefore, brethren, look ye out among you seven men of honest report, full of the Holy Ghost and wisdom, whom we may appoint over this business*" **Acts 6: 3 (KJV)**. **(Emphasis added)**

"*...whom we may appoint over this business*" **v3**.

The nature of the business is well defined. The context of the objectives is well specified. They were to manage both the daily collection and the daily distributions of the charity in such ways that were transparent and impartial to the satisfaction of all who were poor and widows. It was a sensitive task seeing that contention had been brewing from the agitations of the Grecians who claimed that their widows were being marginalized.

The management of the very large daily collections and distributions was no job for just anyone. It required the services of men with confirmed **credibility** and wisdom. Much more, it required the services of men whose life were known to be under the strict discipline of the Holy Spirit. There was absolutely no room for the display of favoritism or sentiments in the choosing of these stewards. It had to be absolutely on the basis of their credentials. They were chosen on the basis of their attributes. Their qualities distinguished them for the assignment.

So, we see that young David was chosen and the Seven Stewards were chosen. They were all chosen because they possessed attributes and qualities that made them worthy. They were all chosen because their antecedents **have** proven them to be valuable assets in the circumstances **at hand.**

Beloved, are you an asset or a liability? Have you proven yourself to be of value to anything at all?

Has there been occasions where you were recommended as the solution to a challenge? What do you consider your credentials in life? What are those qualities that readily distinguish you? You know, it isn't too late to start adding value to your life.

The bible tells us that,

> "A man's gift maketh room for him, and bringeth him before great men" **Proverbs 18: 16 (KJV)**.

The implication of this is that a man's value is what announces him to the world.

The Parable of the Talent teaches us that God loves increase, growth, multiplication, development and productivity.

Work on yourself, develop yourself and become an indispensable valuable asset in the kingdom and to your generation. Maximize your gifts and potentials – covet more gifts. Develop your character. Manage your assets. Use your time valuably. Increase your understanding. Broaden your perspective of life. These will distinguish you in life and grant you access where many have found none.

PRAYER LINE!

Mighty God, I receive grace this hour to add value to my life, that I may be of value to my family, society and generation. Father, dominate my character by Your Spirit – grant me Spirit inspired attributes. By Your Hand upon my life, distinguish me for honor. Amen!

PROPHETIC INTERJECTION

I pray and I decree today in the name of Jesus Christ that my days of servitude in oppression and suppression are over! I decree that my days of aimlessness, barrenness, and impotence are over in Jesus' name. I refuse to have any day of barrenness or miscarriage again in my life! I dismantle the mandate and activities of dark powers contending and postponing my joy, marriage, healing, restoration and lifting from year to year in Jesus' name, Amen!!!

Chapter 3

From Within to Without

Everything in life takes initiative from within. Everything that makes impart begins from within. Everything that grows begin from within. Human biological life begins from within the womb. The vegetation plant begins from within the earth. The fruit of the trees begin from within the seed. Visions are first conceived from within the mind. Creation itself was birthed from within the word of God. Every work of God in the life of a man necessarily begins from within the mind of the man. What the mind cannot conceive cannot be actualized in life. Greatness begins from within the mind.

PRAYER LINE!

Father, I present my life and my heart to you. You know all things, and You search the depths of man's heart. Search me o Lord… And bring to manifestation every gift and ability hidden in my life. Amen!

Now, relating both subject references in the scripture, David the son of Jesse and the Seven Stewards, we see that the choices made of both young David and the Seven Stewards was indeed a call from within.

1 Samuel 16: 18-19 (KJV).

18. *Then answered one of the servants, and said, Behold, I have seen a son of Jesse the Bethlehemite, that is cunning in playing, and a mighty valiant man, and a man of war, and prudent in matters, and a comely person, and the Lord is with him.*

19. *Wherefore Saul sent messengers unto Jesse, and said, Send me David thy son, which is with the sheep.*

A closer look at the above text reveals the very humble state that defined the life of young David at the time of his discovery. The king sent his messengers to Jesse with these words,

> "...*Send me David thy son, which is with the sheep*" **v19**.

Note the emphasis – 'David thy son, which is with the sheep".

We see that David's peculiarity or attributes was not discovered or noticed in beautiful places like in Las Vegas, or Buckingham palace, or the white house, but in the wilderness, where the news of his valiant skills would have reached the ears of the young man who recommended him to the king. It was right there in the wilderness that he defeated the bear and overcame the lions while taking care of his sheep. David mastered his musical notes and psalms in the wilderness which was like a second home for him, while he tended the sheep on a daily basis.

David knew what it **means** to be a victor and a champion right there in the wilderness, not the palace! The wilderness defined his purpose, prepared him for his God given mandate, and qualified him in due time. It was right there in the wilderness that he became a skillful sling user as he gained mastery in the use of the catapult, targeting and bringing down birds from far distance and high altitudes. The wilderness was the **WITHIN** experience for a young shepherd boy like David. Therefore, when the opportunity came **WITHOUT**, he had series of wonderful and excellent performances. The giant Goliath was only similar to the many conquest in the wilderness. David's training **WITHIN** the wilderness, afforded him mastery of his slings and stones. He had gained mastery of precision target in the course of his many application thereof in hunting the birds of the air.

The instrument of the harp he played **WITHOUT** at the presence of the king was mastered **WITHIN** in the wilderness at the presence of no one.

Also in respect to the Seven Stewards, we read:

Acts 6: 1-3 (KJV)

1. *And in those days, when the number of the disciples was multiplied, there arose a murmuring of the Grecians against the Hebrews, because their widows were neglected in the daily ministration.*
2. *Then the twelve called the multitude of the disciples unto them, and said, It is not reason that we should leave the word of God, and serve tables.*
3. *Wherefore, brethren, look ye out among you seven men of honest report, full of the Holy Ghost and wisdom, whom we may appoint over this business.*

Apparently, we see that the selection of the seven was done from **WITHIN** the camp of the congregation.

The twelve apostles commanded the multitudes of the disciples saying,

"...look ye out among you seven men..." v3.

In essence, these men were Known and chosen from within the congregation. Everything begins from **WITHIN!** God the commander-in-chief of the whole universe began the creation first from within before their outward manifestation in the creation story. A baby's growth begins within as an embryo, then fetus till delivery when the growth continues without. When a seed is planted in the ground, the germination and growth of the seed begins within before it develops a shoot without.

As it was with David so it is with the Seven Stewards. These two were first found to be operating in obscurity before they were brought to the limelight. So, if we are going to move from obscurity to prominence, transition to destination, from relegation to **elevation**, and from ruins to rule in life, then we need to understand the **WITHIN** dimension, where we are groomed and fortified with the necessary preparation and training in order to ensure great performance **WITHOUT!**

PRAYER LINE!

Father, I release my heart to the demands of the process. As I wait on, reveal Your plans for my life. Perfect all that is required of my life... As I wait on you, teach me Your ways, deal with my character. Rid me of all stumbling blocks in my life. Amen!

The **WITHIN** dimension is God's pattern of due process in our lives in order to prepare us, and make us robust in the day of our announcing. When God wants to lift a person, He sends a man but when our character becomes a stumbling block, great opportunity fails in our hands. This explains why opportunity must necessarily meet with preparation, otherwise we would fail and disappoint others on the day of our visitation!

OPPORTUNITY + PREPARATION = SUCCESS.

INDUSTRY, NOT FANTASY

We must be very careful of the injurious sermons flying around everywhere today that tells people you will sleep a poor man and wake up a billionaire the next day. The emphasis on material acquisition at all cost as opposed to character molding through due process - FROM **WITHIN TO WITHOUT** - has become the norm in our homes, churches, and the society at large.

For us to understand the foolishness in laziness, we need to closely observe the ant.

Proverbs 6: 6-11 (KJV)

6. *Go to the ant, thou sluggard; consider her ways, and be wise:*

7. *Which having no guide, overseer, or ruler,*

8. *Provideth her meat in the summer, and gathereth her food in the harvest.*

9. *How long wilt thou sleep, O sluggard? when wilt thou arise out of thy sleep?*

10. *Yet a little sleep, a little slumber, a little folding of the hands to sleep:*

11. *So shall thy poverty come as one that travelleth, and thy want as an armed man.*

You see, no one tells the ants what to do. All summer they store up food. At harvest, they stockpile provisions. So how long do you plan to stay lazy, idle and unproductive? How long before you get out of bed? A nap here, a nap there, a day off here, a day off there, sitting back and taking it easy. Beloved, you know what comes next? With such indolence, one can only look forward to a **dirty-poor** life, having poverty as your permanent houseguest.

Industry is what makes you wealthy, not fantasy! I don't know of any frustration or illusion greater than the insanity of folks digging the scriptures daily for reasons to justify unruly lifestyles, perverting God's gift of grace into an overall covering for disorder. If you want to see the authentic finger of God at work in the affairs of men, then go to the sphere where the law of process and character molding is recognized, respected and embraced. Success is not a state, but a commitment to process and its principles.

PRAYER LINE!

My God, I rebuke the spirit of laziness from my life. I declare that I shall not live a wasted life. I receive the zeal to work. And I declare that the works of my hands are blessed... I declare that all my efforts are crowned with success. Amen!

THE DILIGENT ATTRACTS OPPORTUNITY

I dare say that if the biblical order and principles are sought with the same fervor and tenacity that money, power and fame are sought after everywhere today, then we will no doubt birth true kingdom champions that will **stand for Jesus!** Until there is nothing more important to us than seeking first the Kingdom of God and His righteousness, all **these** material blessings we crave for in our prayer rallies and conferences will do us little good.

As we mature in Him, we will become more and more of an asset to Him, then 'every other thing' becomes a natural consequence.

It is amazing and of a notable value to notice that neither was a vote of confidence taken nor was any form of lobbying necessary to determine the **identities** of these seven men chosen to be stewards.

There were neither any form of newspaper advert nor local radio station propaganda, nor yet a head hunting agency hired to facilitate the discovery of persons with the attributes of David and **those** of the Seven Stewards. These referrals came by persons of their environment **whom by** the course of time took keen notice of their competence and proficiency, crowned with humility, diligence, dedication, discipline and character. If you are diligent, disciplined and dedicated to your assignment, the right opportunity will naturally be drawn to you. This is a natural consequence **of** dedication, discipline and diligence. Without these you are neither a formidable reference nor an identifiable asset even in your domain.

It is the desire for excellence and distinction in life that propels the 'would be' champions to stay up late and get up early, sweating it out in the place of training, strategic planning and hard practice. It is the desire for excellence that sees one 'learning', 'unlearning' and 'relearning' on the very competitive global trade. It is the desire for excellence that keeps us pressing. Success is not an accident! Success is the outcome of an unrelenting pursuit and determined conquest of set objectives. Success is the consistent logical act of distinctive combination of processes positioned by a period of invested time through intense dedication and discipline.

THE WORLD IS WATCHING YOU

A newly born-again brother who was so motivated, vibrant and enthused by the reality of the power of the Gospel in his daily life went out to evangelize his former neighborhood gang members. His new-found life, peace and happiness kept him pushing and pressing on his friends to receive Christ but the gang leader who also was his best friend kept giving him a particular excuse that he was very busy reading a book, but would visit his Jesus when he was done reading that book. This continued for months until one day, almost at the time this young brother had given up hope of converting his friends.

He was seated at the front row of his local fellowship and bewildered as he saw his former gang members walk up to answer the altar call. At the end of the service the young brother rushed down to his best friend and demanded to know what on earth could have been responsible for this great miracle, the gang leader responded "the book!" "What book?" he asked.

He explained that the book he had been reading all this time was his own life. He observed him to affirm that his claims to a new life was sustained in his character. He read his friend all these months to ascertain for himself first hand if truly indeed, he really was changed.

My dearly beloved brethren in Christ Jesus, the moral of this short story is that by the virtues of our new status in Christ Jesus, we,

> "...are manifestly declared to be the epistle of Christ ministered by us, written not with ink, but with the Spirit of the living God; not in tables of stone, but in fleshy tables of the heart" **2Corinthian 3: 3 (KJV)**.

Our profession of the Faith puts us in the spot light. We become known and read of all men, that we may shine forth the light of the Kingdom in a fallen and depraved world.

PRAYER LINE!

My God and My Father, I repent of every lifestyle that has passed the wrong message to the watching world. I ask your forgiveness... Help me to live the truth. Help me to live as the light that I am. Help me to be the Jesus Christ the world sees. Help me dear Lord. Amen!

God is looking to see a generation of saints that are minded to represent the core values of the kingdom in all sincerity of faith. God is looking to see men and women whose reputable character places a distinction on them as children of God. God is looking to find men and women whose gestures perfectly models His intent for the church. Both David and the Seven Stewards were men who represented God in their generation. It is no wonder they were distinguished. Men and women who represent God to every generation are sought after. When our character, virtues and values reflect the God in us, our generation cannot but reckon to us every due honor.

AS THE WORLD GETS DARKER, THE TRUE CHURCH AND THE SONS OF GOD WILL SHINE BRIGHTER AND BRIGHTER UNTO THE PERFECT DAY - AMEN!

"A good name is rather to be chosen than great riches, and loving favour rather than silver and gold" **Proverbs 22: 1 (KJV)**.

◫―PROPHETIC INTERJECTION

I decree and declare today by the authority in the name of Jesus, anything in me that co-operates with unrighteousness, limitation, affliction and frustration expires this hour in Jesus' name! Any form of wickedness, idolatory and way of life in me limiting the move of God in my life from year to year drops off now by fire, in Jesus' name, Amen!

Chapter 4

From Isolation to Recomendation

I already spoke about recommendation earlier but something in these verses yet call for attention.

> "Then answered one of the servants, and said, Behold, I have seen a son of Jesse the Bethlehemite, that is cunning in playing, and a mighty valiant man, and a man of war, and prudent in matters, and a comely person, and the Lord is with him" **1Samuel 16: 18 (KJV).**

And

> "Wherefore, brethren, look ye out among you seven men of honest report, full of the Holy Ghost and wisdom, whom we may appoint over this business" **Acts 6: 3 (KJV).**

In the former verse, we see that the playing skills of young David **was so good, acknowledged, and were highlighted as a notable potential of his.** In spite of his humble disposition as a shepherd boy, and the challenging task of shepherding, as well as all the odds of the wilderness life, **yet, he gained** successful mastery of his **playing skills.**

In the later verse, we reckon that in spite of the excellent profiles that distinguished these seven men, they were willing to stay committed in service as a team, humbly serving in the distribution of charity to the poor and widows – with a lowly heart, serving tables!

Beloved, the point is this; the challenges of life are nothing but programmed opportunities to stretch our faith beyond the pain, shame and stain of our overwhelming circumstances. Our faith must thrive and flourish above the odds of life in order to frustrate what we see to the point that it bows to what we believe. Those who desire to change history and shameful circumstances must be willing to embrace uncommon lifestyle.

PRAYER LINE!

Father, open my heart to the lessons I must learn in my present circumstance. Teach me the lessons that are key for my future. I receive faith to persevere through these times. I receive strength to press on. Amen!

Abraham was called a Hebrew, **Genesis 14: 13**. Meaning 'man from beyond'; the implication of what he was called suggested that he was a man who demonstrated an unusual kind of faith. The reason he was called this is that faith is from the world BEYOND.

Grace, obedience, humility, purity, good success, His manifest presence and glory are all from a world called BEYOND - beyond human reasoning, beyond natural ability. Friends, <u>**it takes something**</u> that is definitely beyond the carnal mind and human strength of Abraham **to pursue**, overtake, defeat **and annihilate** a total number of five enemy kings together with their legions of soldiers with only three hundred and eighteen house trained servants - servants who had never been to war, who had neither military background nor training, who had no advantage of modern military weaponry and ammunition. It is beyond his human mind that he staggered not at the promise of God through unbelief; but was strong in faith, giving glory to God; and being fully persuaded that, what God had promised, He was able also to perform it BEYOND our imagination and natural minds.

> *"But the natural man receiveth not the things of the Spirit of God: for they are foolishness unto him: neither can he know them, because they are spiritually discerned"*
> **1Corinthians 2: 14 (KJV)**.

NOW LETS GO BEYOND!

SORROW OF TRAVIAL – JOY OF DELIVERY

Please realize that it is not where you are in life that actually matters, Success is not dependent on geographical location, but divine allocation. It is not your present status in the society that determines your success potentials, it is rather your status in God that makes the difference. It is not the size of your bank account that give prerequisite for success, it is rather the faith in your spirit that precipitates great accomplishments.

Don't allow what you lack at the moment to label you to the extent that it frustrates your values and your resolve for determined accomplishments and success. Beloved, do not allow the pressures and challenges arising from the present lack and scarcity push you to that point where you begin to compromise on honesty, fidelity, morality, trustworthiness, sincerity, uprightness, virtue, responsibility, incorruptibility, integrity and credibility. Pride and vainglory have robbed many today of their colorful destiny in Christ Jesus. Hear me; you are not what you wear, where you live, and what you drive! Never allow vanity and vapors dictate the volume, value and extent of your reputation within your sphere of influence. Our Lord Jesus imperatively warned against greed.

> *"...Take heed, and beware of covetousness: for a man's life consisteth not in the abundance of the things which he possesseth"* **Luke 12: 15 (KJV).**

The man whose treasure is found in character and rooted at the teachings of Jesus Christ will most certainly rule in the midst of his enemies. That man who follows after the steps of Christ Jesus will ultimately have all oppositions trodden underfoot. He who walks with Christ can never be restrained by the presence of adversaries.

You see, pain and gain is the cycle of life which even faith cannot disrupt. But pain loses out when honesty, integrity and good report becomes the focus. Nothing really jolts the word-based approach to life and its events. Pain is forgotten when gain follows. The worse the journey is, the sweeter the arrival. Whatever can't stop God from arriving at purpose, must give up on our appointed time and season of overflowing gain. When we live our lives with the mindset of projecting the character and integrity of the Gospel of the Kingdom of God, God likewise commits Himself to the delivery of His purpose for our lives. The pain of the process compulsorily gives way to the joy of great accomplishments.

John 16: 21-22 (KJV).

21. *A woman when she is in travail hath sorrow, because her hour is come: but as soon as she is delivered of the child, she remembereth no more the anguish, for joy that a man is born into the world.*

22. *And ye now therefore have sorrow: but I will see you again, and your heart shall rejoice, and your joy no man taketh from you.*

THE SUCCESS OF CHARACTER

We are the ambassadors of enviable report endowed and graced with a functional reality of the power of the Gospel that will endear the heathen asking: "...*whose son is this youth?*" **1Samuel 17: 55 (KJV)**. Even at this time and age where everything is technologically and scientifically doctored and micro waved, the power of the Gospel at work in our lives continue to prove superior to everyone and to everything.

Our Christian walk and life should generate the character reputation, as well as the persevering passion that will qualify us to be the SOUGHT AFTER in our given domains and sphere of influence. We have a responsibility to let the world see the physical manifestation of the culture, influence and intentions of the Father in a world that is forever ready and willing to mock and criticize the church of our living Christ. You see, greatness, excellence, diligence and character work hand in hand, they are likened to a tree trapped in a seed, as we already know that trees are not in the soil but a hidden deposit in a seed. Hence, we are seeds sent into the world to produce a tree and serve our fruits to the world. This is a service revealed only in the place of humility and character. Nobody, no matter how intelligent succeeds beyond the boundaries of his character!

Godly character is developed when we allow God write his law in our hearts by His Spirit. And we make conscious efforts to bring our daily dispositions <u>in</u> subjection to the demands of the Holy Spirit. But the dictionary defines character as 'moral excellence and firmness.' The main standard of character is typified in the bible. Character is illustrated in Jesus Christ. It's no wonder He made a success of His earthly ministry. It is written that *"pride goeth before destruction, and an haughty spirit before a fall"* **Proverbs 16: 18 (KJV)**. Many have often said that "humility precipitates honor." But I dare say that "character delivers success!"

Holy Spirit, I lay at the altar of your Holy presence... work on my heart Lord. Remove from me all things that offends Your presence. Mortify my flesh – break me, and remold me to whom you want me to be. Let my life please you. Amen!

But men don't build Christian character overnight. Like every other thing of great price, character is developed but through processes requiring our commitment. But what you will not commit yourself to, you can never achieve. Commitment is key to attainment. Commitment is obligatory in some sense, meaning that our commitment to a course necessarily obligates us to same course. Commitment to anything at all takes of our devoted time and energy; so, it is with commitment to character development. It requires our conscious effort, we must be devoted to working with the indwelling Spirit of God in His intention of molding us into the character that presents us as the children of God that we indeed are. Commitment to character development demands our conscious and deliberate effort to remain under the discipline of the Holy Spirit.

All who have received the grace of God in Christ Jesus have also received the indwelling presence of the Holy Spirit. But not all who have received the Spirit have yielded to the discipline of the Spirit. The wonderful intent for which the Spirit indwells the child of God may not come to full light until the child of God willfully submits to the **wholistic** influence of the Spirit. Therefore, Commitment to Christian character building demands that we remain open to the rebukes and chastisement of the Holy Spirit; humbling ourselves under His influence as He breaks us in reprimand, prunes us of all excesses, and smoothen all rough edges. Christian Character is essentially necessary.

> *"That ye would walk worthy of God, who hath called you unto his kingdom and glory"*
> **1 Thessalonians 2: 12 (KJV).**

▣ PROPHETIC INTERFECTION

Today, I pray and confess that from this moment of my life, I have also become a recipient of divine help that will position me for a ground-breaking testimony that begets unending chains of uncommon testimonies in, Jesus' name. I insist that the work which His goodness began in my life, the arm of his strength shall complete, to His glory, in Jesus' name. Amen!

Chapter 5

Full Of The Holy Spirit

It is commonly agreed, given all antecedents of God's dealing with man, that the presence of God in a man's life makes the most difference. No one in whose life God was evidently present was ever known to live an ordinary life. No one who carried God's presence lived a meaningless or wasted life. Success, accomplishment and fulfillment are the hallmark of the presence of God in the life of anyone.

Again, a reference is made to our topical scriptures:

> "Then answered one of the servants, and said, Behold, I have seen a son of Jesse the Bethlehemite, that is cunning in playing, and a mighty valiant man, and a man of war, and prudent in matters, and a comely person, and the Lord is with him" **1Samuel 16: 18 (KJV)**.

> "Wherefore, brethren, look ye out among you seven men of honest report, full of the Holy Ghost and wisdom, whom we may appoint over this business" **Acts 6: 3 (KJV)**.

We consider that it was reported of David that,

"...the Lord is with him"

and also of the Seven Stewards that they are,

"...full of the Holy Ghost..."

There is a parallel of the two scriptures **above I wish** to bring before us. The testimony of David was that THE LORD WAS WITH HIM. But the question is, what did it mean **for** David **to have the Lord be with him?** It simply means that the Spirit of God was upon him. This understanding brings to light the parallel between *"...the LORD was with him..."* and *"full of the Holy Ghost"* - because both statements actually mean the same thing. Having the Lord with you as in the case of David is to be full of the Spirit as in the case of the Seven Stewards.

The seven were FULL OF THE HOLY GHOST which made them divinely empowered for the business assigned to them. David also had THE LORD WITH HIM which made him a mighty valiant man, a man of war. Truth is, you cannot be full of the HOLY GHOST and remain empty or ordinary. The infilling of God's Spirit automatically qualifies you for supernatural exploits. The presence of God capacitates you to achieve great things - things beyond human comprehension. When the Lord is with you, you become extraordinary in your dealings and approaches, you become a warrior and mighty things would be done through you by the almighty God!

PRAYER LINE!

Father, fill my life again with Your Spirit. Fill me to overflowing... I Hunger for Your presence. Revive my spirit again. Set me on fire for You. With my hands lifted to heaven, I receive the Power of Your Spirit. Amen!

It is important to note here that the measure of God's power and presence in a believer's life is dependent on how much his life is ordered by the SPIRIT. The key of absolute obedience and holy living makes the believer unmanageable to the devil and his cohort. If you connect to the invisible, the impossible becomes laughable – yes! The call to salvation is not about eternal bliss and security alone. The call to salvation is a call to experience the command of supernatural abilities confrontations.

The call to salvation is a call to know Him who has called you, and to come to a comprehension of His plans for your life. The call to salvation is a call to serve the extraordinary intents of the supernatural God. You did not get saved to live eternal life alone, you got saved to conquer the world for Jesus. You got saved to demonstrate a life of signs and wonders.

> "Behold, I and the children whom the Lord hath given me are for signs and for wonders in Israel from the Lord of hosts, which dwelleth in mount Zion" **Isaiah 8: 18 (KJV).**

MAY OUR UNDERSTANDING BE ENLIGHTENED

Beloved, I pray the Lord, that as you read through the inspired lines of this literature, that,

> "the eyes of your understanding being enlightened; that ye may know what is the hope of his calling, and what the riches of the glory of his inheritance in the saints" **Ephesians 1:18 (KJV).**

The disconcerting confrontations opposing the blissful manifestations of God's children arises from a very poor knowledge of whom they are, and what they have. The majority of believers today are grossly unaware of the divine authority vested on them as the seed of divinity – born of God. Many have remained ignorant of the potentials embedded in them as regenerated beings. Thus, Paul prayed, like I am praying right now, that:

> *"the eyes of your understanding being enlightened..."*

When the LORD appears, we achieve the incredible and possess the unimaginable; we do the impossible because we are both touching and are being touched by the intangible power of God through our faith and our walk in the Spirit. When the Spirit of the Lord is in you, you become a time bomb of greatness going places to explode for God. You become a very dangerous person against the host of Hades. You do things differently, and your difference is very visible even without announcing it. When the Spirit of the Lord came upon King Saul, he did what he had never done before; he prophesied even in the midst of the prophets. When the Spirit of the Lord came upon David, he also prophesied in the midst of prophets.

1Samuel 10: 6-7 (KJV)

6. *And the Spirit of the Lord will come upon thee, and thou shalt prophesy with them, and shalt be turned into another man.*
7. *And let it be, when these signs are come unto thee, that thou do as occasion serve thee; for God is with thee.*

Samuel anointed Saul and kissed him, and told him he would come to Gibeah of God, where there was a Philistine garrison. Samuel explained that as Saul approached the town, he would run into a company of prophets coming down from the shrine, and playing the harps and tambourines, flutes and drums, these prophets would be prophesying. Then Samuel noted that the Spirit of God would come on Saul as well, and he would prophesy together with the prophets. And HE WOULD BE TRANSFORMED, **becoming a new person!** In Samuel's words:

> *"And let it be, when these signs are come unto thee, that thou do as occasion serve thee; for God is with thee"* **1Samuel 10: 7 (KJV)**.

Saul's prophetic bond with the company of prophets was to be a sign for him that he had been endowed with ability to do the job set before him because God was now with him.

SUPERNATURAL ABILITIES BY THE SPIRIT

When the Spirit of God came upon Saul he was turned into another man:

1Samuel 10: 5-6 (KJV)

5. *After that thou shalt come to the hill of God, where is the garrison of the Philistines: and it shall come to pass, when thou art come thither to the city, that thou shalt meet a company of prophets coming down from the high place with a psaltery, and a tabret, and a pipe, and a harp, before them; and they shall prophesy:*

6. *And the Spirit of the Lord will come upon thee, and thou shalt prophesy with them, and shalt be turned into another man.*

The Spirit of the Lord in the life of a man primarily serves to **make supernatural the natural abilities of that man.** The Spirit of the Lord is the personal expression of the capacity of the Almighty God. God indwells us in the person of His Spirit. Everything God intends for our individual lives are the same things He looks to accomplish in us through the person of His Spirit in us. The assumption that man in his natural state has what it takes to accomplish divine purpose is on the one hand a gross underestimation of the standards of divinity, and on the second hand an overestimation of man's degenerated nature. God gives us His Spirit to qualify and certify us for the accomplishments of His divine objectives for our individual lives. Without His Spirit in us, we can accomplish nothing for God.

When God is with you, you must be transformed, you become a brand-new person, not necessarily a better version of yourself. When God is with you, and His Spirit in your life, you would become a sign to your generation and you would become a living proof of God's miracle working power – Amen!

PRAYER LINE!

Father, as I receive Your Spirit afresh right now, I declare that I am turned into another man. I receive supernatural endowment – I receive supernatural abilities. Amen!

Friends, God is the fountain of all that is possible in life, there's a place in Him where ALL HE IS can flow through you unhindered beyond the borders of your **inadequacy and distress to the light of the needy world.** All you need to do is to make yourself available to this able God who alone **could** do great wonders, even with the physically challenged, so that all glory forever **belongs** to Him and Him alone – Amen!

▭— PROPHETIC INTERJECTION

In the name of Jesus Christ, I pray and decree that from this moment of my life, never again shall I end a day biting my fingers in disappointment, despair and frustration! Come what may, evil must miss its mark in my life on all fronts, in Jesus' name, Amen!!!

Chapter 6

Divine Wisdom - Prudent In Matters

Thus far, we have seen some very profound light in the connecting lines between these two situations in the bible. We have been enlightened by the revelations proceeding from the characteristic features that distinguished both young David and the Seven Stewards. Their esteemed merits endorsed them for the tasks, **uncontested and unopposed.** They were certified by all, verified by all, and attested **to** by all. They were simply indisputable! Their personal attributes put them in a class that was beyond question. Again, from the reference scriptures we also find yet another thought-provoking parallel **with** young David and the Seven Stewards.

> *"Then answered one of the servants, and said, Behold, I have seen a son of Jesse the Bethlehemite, that is cunning in playing, and a mighty valiant man, and a man of war, and prudent in matters, and a comely person, and the Lord is with him"* **1Samuel 16: 18 (KJV).**

"Wherefore, brethren, look ye out among you seven men of honest report, full of the Holy Ghost and wisdom, whom we may appoint over this business" **Acts 6:3 (KJV).**

Let's kindly dwell on these two phrases:

"...prudent in matter..." **1Samuel 16: 18 (KJV).**

And

"...and wisdom..." **Acts 6: 3 (KJV).**

The two scriptures above are communicating the same thing: WISDOM!

Wisdom is a special ingredient that is seen to be possessed by great people trans-generationally. Wisdom has made many stand-out amongst their contemporaries, as is the case of David, a valiant and courageous man who is PRUDENT IN MATTERS; as well as the Seven Stewards, who are full of WISDOM, and **endowed** with both competence and intelligence.

It is commonly quoted:

Proverbs 8: 11-12 (KJV)

11. *For wisdom is better than rubies; and all the things that may be desired are not to be compared to it.*

12. *I wisdom dwell with prudence, and find out knowledge of witty inventions.*

THE SUPERIORITY OF WISDOM

The place of wisdom is superior to anything and everything that may be the object of man's greatest desire. The superiority of wisdom to all of man's earthly pursuits is not undermined in the Holy Scripture. Simply put, wisdom is God's way of doing things. And we know that God's way of doing things has proven to be eternally result oriented and excellently productive. Wisdom is the mind of God – wisdom is the expression of the mind of God. This is yet another function of the indwelling presence of the Holy Spirit. The Spirit of God in us looks to fashion our minds after the wisdom of God.

Giving the help of the Holy Spirit, God expects to have you develop wisdom,

> *"…by the renewing of your mind, that ye may prove what is that good, and acceptable, and perfect, will of God"* **Romans 12: 2 (KJV).**

Without controversy, we all can quickly agree that it can only take a mind that has been renewed after the wisdom of God to prove what is good, acceptable and perfect. It takes a mind of wisdom to know the will of God in every given situation. Consequently, James tells the church:

> *"If any of you lack wisdom, let him ask of God, that giveth to all men liberally, and upbraideth not; and it shall be given him"*
> **James 1: 5 (KJV)**.

Beloved, when was the last time you asked the Lord for His wisdom?

Wisdom says of herself;

> *"...I wisdom dwell with prudence..."*
> **Proverbs 8: 12 (KJV)**.

While prudence is defined as being judicious, wisdom is practical. **True wisdom corresponds with action.** The corresponding actions of wisdom will always lead to the achievement of best results by using the most appropriate means. So, we see how it is that wisdom is the prudent practical application of both knowledge and understanding. It's no wonder she proudly says of herself,

> *"...I wisdom dwell with prudence..."*

Indeed, she does!

The further wisdom proceeds in man, the more he acquaints with excellence. As wisdom is gained, excellence is reflected. It suffices to learn that wisdom produces excellent results – the God kind of results.

No wonder wisdom is called THE PRINCIPAL THING that even God the creator of the universe **had to by this same wisdom made the heavens and laid the foundations of** the earth upon the waters, separating waters from waters in the beginning of beginnings.

PRAYER LINE!

Father, this day I ask for wisdom. I refuse to continue with the wisdom of men. I reject the wisdom of this world. My God, I receive Your wisdom... Henceforth, may my life be directed by Your wisdom. Amen!

Christ our Lord is not left out in the book of wisdom. We learn that He grew in wisdom.

> *"And the child grew, and waxed strong in spirit, filled with wisdom: and the grace of God was upon him"* **Luke 2: 40 (KJV)**.

He grew in both wisdom 'spiritual' and in stature 'physical'. All the prophets of Old Testament and the apostles of the New Testament at different times in different generation operated in this divine attribute called wisdom. What about the kings, among whom Solomon stood out because God gave him a blank cheque and the entire figure Solomon could fill in this cheque was WISDOM. It is no wonder he stood out among kings mentioned in the bible, and even in the history of humanity!

THREE CLASSES OF WISDOM

The Christian operates on three kinds of Wisdom. The Christian equipment in Wisdom is a many-sided thing. There is the wisdom, **Sophia,** a Greek word which the word "sophisticated" is gotten from. This kind of wisdom talks about prudence, magnificence, splendor and it is most common in the religious settings, **it is which sees the ultimate truths of God.**

Phronesis is another kind of wisdom a Christian can operate in, this is known as the practical wisdom, which makes you see what ought to be done in any particular situation.

The third one is **Sunesis** which is a critical and analytical wisdom that can assess and evaluate every course of action which presents itself.

The Christian is not only the dreamer whose thoughts are long, **who is** detached from this world. The Christian is not only a shrewd evaluator of any policy or **any** situation. The Christian is all three. The Christian has not only the vision to know God, but he also has the practical knowledge and ability to turn that vision into action, and the sound judgment to see what course of action **will** best achieve his aim. Although divine wisdom is not necessarily the discovery of the mind, however it cannot be obtained without the strenuous activity of the mind.

Divine wisdom comes when the Spirit of God reaches down to meet the searching mind of man, but the mind of man must search, before God will come to meet it. Wisdom is not for the mentally lazy even though it is the gift of God. Divine wisdom was a creative ingredient in the **creation of the universe**. So, Wisdom was there in the beginning because wisdom was resident in God, and this same wisdom, which has God's imaginative power, with the capacity to cause a creative ability, was transferred into MAN when he became a living soul due to God's INSPIRATION (the breath of God).

MAN was living in God's wisdom and by God's wisdom, until they 'romanced' the Tree of Knowledge of both Good and Evil, and they became

KNOWLEDGEABLY AWARE of everything around them, ranging from good to evil. Man's divine inspirational wisdom therefore became PERVERTED with falsified information.

This corrupt wisdom now made man to KNOW that the serpent is a deceiver, which they never knew before while the serpent was both 'seducing' and 'tempting' them. This corrupt wisdom now made man to hide from God's voice, **instead of fellowship with Him.**

This corrupt wisdom now made man to **become** wise in their own eyes, so they saw for the first time, their creative ability by weaving fig leaves in other to make clothes from the 'fig boutique' for themselves without God's help. Sad! Although God removed that creativity from their bodies and replaced it with a better **one** (animal skin), to show man that they would always need His help, in spite of their new-found wisdom. This corrupt wisdom started the blame game, where no man wants to take responsibility for any evil done.

So, we see that while God's manifold wisdom inspired the MAN to exercise DOMINION, the corrupt wisdom of this world teaches mankind to DOMINATE **themselves to their injury!** The first world war and second world wars are a typical example of how mankind has dominated **themselves to their injury,** with ungodly wisdom to destroy themselves, and sophisticated wisdom like that of Albert Einstein in the atomic bomb which was a weapon of mass destruction.

While divine wisdom teaches man to depend on God, worldly wisdom teaches man that they can do without God. I could go on and on. What I'm saying in encapsulation is, there's a DISTINCTION between DIVINE WISDOM and WORLDLY WISDOM.

There's nothing wrong with science, technology, psychology and philosophy. And as a matter of truth, these are **iota** display or function of God's manifold wisdom, but they could become wrong or WORLDLY if they go against God. Understand that the word 'science' is derived from the Greek verb 'Scire' which means to find out in order to know. In this sense, Adam and Eve exhibited a corrupt 'Scire' in the beginning as they wanted to find out in order to know about what was forbidden. Science is the progenitor of Technology which is from the combination of two Greek words 'Teknon' which means 'to beget' and 'Logos' which means to study. Philosophy is from 'Philo' which means to love or have affinity for something and 'Sophia' which means wisdom, magnificence or prudence. So, we can simply **say** that philosophy is an affinity for prudence or wisdom. Psychology is also from two words; 'Pseuche' which means soul, or mind and we already know what 'logy' means.

Now, I am not by any means inferring that science, technology, philosophy or psychology are evil or bad in themselves, but the mind of the persons in whose hands they are determines if they turn out good or evil. That's a third-party factor. They all stand as creative agents in this world and we need them TEMPORARILY for humanity's co-existence and harmony. Nevertheless, God's divine wisdom transcends all these, because they were not there in the beginning when WISDOM was in full expression and demonstration as the creative agent in the course of creation.

Finally, the wisdom of this world is a body of wisdom that focuses on this world and nothing beyond. It can be found in men anywhere in any field, and it is mostly selfish and carnal because it is solely about things we can attain in this world and never about things beyond. The wisdom of this world is of no eternal profit. It is **totally** minded on the things of this world alone.

Colossians 3: 1-2 (KJV)

1. *If ye then be risen with Christ, seek those things which are above, where Christ sitteth on the right hand of God.*
2. *Set your affection on things above, not on things on the earth.*

THE WISDOM OF GOD

The wisdom of God comes into effect **to promote a mindedness for the things above.** The wisdom of God is demonstrated for the furtherance of the Kingdom of God. The wisdom of God is directed by the Spirit of God with the purpose of advancing the will of God to the glory of God. But the wisdom of this world stands opposed to everything that is of the Spirit of God,

> *"This wisdom descendeth not from above, but is earthly, sensual, devilish"* **James 3:15 (KJV)**.

We read also:

1Corinthians 1: 20-21 (KJV)

20. *Where is the wise? where is the scribe? where is the disputer of this world? hath not God made foolish the wisdom of this world?*

21. *For after that in the wisdom of God the world by wisdom knew not God, it pleased God by the foolishness of preaching to save them that believe.*

Because the wisdom of this world is inspired by worldly passions, this wisdom can neither promote the mind of God nor advance the kingdom of God. This wisdom cannot know God. The apostle Paul, in his first letter to the Corinthian church explained the way God works and **most powerfully as it turns out.** God has His ways of making worldly wisdom stupid, revealing the **quack** and futility of experts in their conventional wisdom.

So where can you find someone truly wise, truly educated, truly intelligent in this day and age? Has not God exposed it all as pretentious nonsense? Since the world in all her fancy wisdom remain clueless in matters pertaining to the knowledge of God, God in His wisdom took delight in using what the world considered foolishness, the preaching of the gospel, to bring those who put their trust in Him into the way of salvation.

Wisdom remains KEY in the life of the child of God. You cannot provoke supernatural upgrade in your life without wisdom. There is therefore the need to have constant fellowship with the Holy Spirit of God who alone is the giver of divine wisdom. Again, our attention is called to the words of James:

> *"If any of you lack wisdom, let him ask of God, that giveth to all men liberally, and upbraideth not; and it shall be given him"* **James 1:5 (KJV).**

PRAYER LINE!

By the Holy Spirit, I receive the wisdom that unlocks the door for supernatural upgrade in my life. I receive the wisdom I need to command supernatural manifestations. Amen!

◧ PROPHETIC ANTIDOTE

Today, by faith I lift up my staff of prayer in righteousness this hour, and I decree and declare that I will not fall, fail or falter in every area of life's demand, in Jesus' name. Help from above shall locate me, defend me, deliver me, and accompany me to the desired victory from this moment of my life, in Jesus' name, Amen!!!

Chapter

Responsible Service

From our topical scriptural references, we alight again on yet another peculiarity that distinguishes both the persons of young David and the Seven Stewards. These persons were men in whose lives were found the heart and passion for service. They were men known to have great enthusiasm for the wellbeing of others. Again, we consider our reference scriptures.

> "Wherefore Saul sent messengers unto Jesse, and said, Send me David thy son, which is with the sheep" **1Samuel 16: 19 (KJV)**.

And

> "Wherefore, brethren, look ye out among you seven men of honest report, full of the Holy Ghost and wisdom, whom we may appoint over this business" **Acts 6: 3 (KJV)**.

With keen observation, we see the corresponding similitude of essence in the above scriptures. We also see the connectivity of purpose as regarding the **choice** of David and the **choosing** of the Seven Stewards respectively. They were chosen to render SERVICE.

For David, apart from being a comely person or proper in appearance, and the Lord being with him, we can tell he was already used to a life of responsibility and service. Taking care of the sheep, and taking responsibility for the wellbeing and protection of the sheep on a daily basis was an apt display of **his** responsible service. Not only was he in service, he also took responsibility for the purpose for which he served. He served his family by **shepherding** the sheep in the wilderness. He took responsibility for **the** lives and security of the sheep under his **watch and care.**

From his childhood, David had been living a life of responsibility and service, and when it was time for him to upgrade in service, the rise from the wilderness to the king's palace, he was identified by the king as THE ONE WHO TAKES RESPONSIBILITY FOR THE SHEEP.

> *"...Send me David thy son, which is with the sheep"* **1Samuel 16: 19 (KJV).**

We need to understand that we can't be known for being idle or doing nothing. **Nobody ever reckons**

anything with an idle or unoccupied man. We would only be known for what we do or what we are responsible for. That is as simple and honest as it is! Graham Bell is responsible for telephone invention in 1846. Thomas Edison is responsible for the electric bulb invention among several other great inventions. The Wright brothers are responsible for the invention of airplane in 1903. George Frederick Handel is responsible for the popular Hallelujah Chorus.

There are so many examples of people who decided to become responsible, **who** rendered trans-generational services which outlived them. They are long gone but what they have done for humanity remains and can never be forgotten.

PRAYER LINE!

My Father, order my steps along the path of service. Reveal Your plans concerning my life... Direct my heart on where to serve – how to serve – with whom I must serve. Teach me the ways I must serve. Amen!

David's upgrade to serve at the king's palace did not meet him unprepared because he was used to serving even in obscurity.

The seven men who were chosen to serve tables were appointed over this business because overtime they had built a reputation that spoke for them as being responsible enough to meet the needs of this office **without a vacuum.**

Many people today do not want to serve and do not like to be responsible. We have a generation of people who want to be at the top, who want to occupy high offices and secured positions, but are unwilling to serve. Hey! It does not work that way. You cannot find yourself in the king's palace if you are not service oriented. Everyone desires greatness but no one likes to serve. Yet truth remains that service does not just lead to greatness, service itself is greatness!

We often want a BREAKTHROUGH – but we do not like to GO THROUGH that which has been designed by divine arrangement **of process to prepare us for the breakthrough when it comes so that we can handle it.** Serving is an honorable thing; and being responsible is noble.

THE IMPETUS OF SERVICE

Serving **might as well** mean a whole lot of things to people depending on their backgrounds, experiences and discipline. And while the different perspective to serving may not all come in perfect resemblance, there are certain features that necessarily defines true service. The impetus of service takes it cue from the words of Jesus Christ.

> "*Even as the Son of man came not to be ministered unto, but to minister, and to give his life a ransom for many*" **Matthew 20: 28 (KJV)**.

Let us consider the subject of serving from the motivation of Jesus Christ who is our principle role model in all kingdom life affairs. What do we mean when we speak in respect of service? Essentially, we mean the giving of oneself.

We read above that the Lord came,

> "*...to minister, and to give his life a ransom for many*" **Matthew 20: 28 (KJV)**.

The word rendered 'minister' above is derived from the Greek word 'diakoneo' (dee-ak-on-eh'-o), which means 'to be an attendant', 'to wait upon' or 'to serve'. Apparently, the word rendered 'minister' simply means 'to serve'. The Lord Jesus says He came to serve and to give His life a ransom. From this we deduce that the kingdom ideology of serving is simply giving. When we serve, we give. If we are not giving, we are not known to be serving. Kingdom service primarily means the giving of ourselves – our time, our gifts, our resources, our energy, and all that we have. The spending of ourselves for the benefit of others is the essence of service from a kingdom perspective.

Jesus points His disciples to Himself for an example.

Philippians 2: 6-7 (KJV)

6. *Who, being in the form of God, thought it not robbery to be equal with God:*

7. *But made himself of no reputation, and took upon him the form of a servant, and was made in the likeness of men.*

Our Lord "...*made himself of no reputation, and took upon him the form of a servant.*"

He did not come with splendor and grandeur, but condescending to the place of man, He accepted the humble life. And as man, He had not required them to serve Him; but rather, **for them** He laid down His life. He modeled out true kingdom service for us all. Ultimately, He served by giving Himself – His life!

THE SERVICE OF LOVE

Love is the foundation of service. True service is necessary inspired by love, motivated by love, driven by love and sustained in love. True service is made perfect and crowned in love. Where love is absent the essence of service is denied, and the spirit of service is **defeated**. Again, the model for kingdom service is Jesus Christ, and His service to us. We know that Jesus served in love. His service was inspired by love, because He gave Himself in love. We read in His own words;

> "Greater love hath no man than this, that a man lay down his life for his friends" **John 15:13 (KJV).**

The true substance of love is proven in the place of service. The giving of Himself, and more so, His own life, gave substance to His claim of love.

"…*Greater love hath no man than this…*" – laying down His life for the ransom of sinful men was the apex of all **proofs.** He came in love. He dwelt in love. He taught in love. He healed in love. He gave in love. He offered Himself in love. He served for love!

> "And walk in love, as Christ also hath loved us, and hath given himself for us an offering and a sacrifice to God for a sweetsmelling savour" **Ephesians 5: 2 (KJV).**

Again, we see that Christ *"...hath loved us, and hath given himself for us..."* – He loved us, and He gave Himself for us. In His love, He gave. In His love, He served. The service by which He gave of Himself for our ransom was in the demonstration of His love for us. Furthermore, the Lord also commanded us to employ same service of love. The Lord commanded us to give of ourselves; more importantly, to give of ourselves in love.

John 15: 12-13 (KJV)

12. *This is my commandment, That ye love one another, as I have loved you.*

13. *Greater love hath no man than this, that a man lay down his life for his friends.*

The commandment of the Lord to us is *"...That ye love one another, as I have loved you."* And how exactly has He loved us? He has loved us by laying down His life for our good. He has loved us by sacrificing of Himself for our wellbeing. He has loved us by emptying of Himself that we may be full in ourselves. He has loved us by serving our interest. And now, He commands us to love others as He has loved us. John puts it this way:

> *"Hereby perceive we the love of God, because he laid down his life for us: and we ought to lay down our lives for the brethren"* **1 John 3: 16 (KJV).**

PRAYER LINE!

My God and My Father, I receive the grace to love as Jesus loved. I receive the spirit to serve as He served. Give me a heart and a passion to serve You with my life, and to serve others in love. Amen!

Because Christ gave in love, laying down His life for us, John exhorts us to give of ourselves in same spirit – the spirit of love. We are called to lay down our lives for the wellbeing of others. We are called to pursue the interest of others over and above our own interests. We are called to make personal sacrifices for the good of others. We are called to follow the examples of Christ; not just to serve but to serve in the spirit of love.

We ought always to be ready to make the required sacrifices in serving the interest of others. And how else is this sacrificial 'service call' a logical reality except it be inspired by the love of God in our hearts for mankind? It could only take love to make certain kind of sacrifices. The love which led our Savior to sacrifice His life for our good, should lead us to do the same thing for our brethren and neighbors. If circumstances should require it. Love knows no borders.

Because our Lord gave Himself in love, we must thus do likewise. Serving is sourced from the spirit of true love. As we serve in love the burden of the demands and sacrifices of service becomes easily bearable. Where love thrives, **dwell no burden.** Love conquers all! **Because** we love, we serve with the right heart, and the right attitude. **Because** we love, our service emits the fragrance of love. **Because** we love, the joy of service overflows from our hearts; what remains tough and strenuous for others becomes for us a mere demonstration of kingdom benevolence. Again, love conquers all!

▭━PROPHETIC INTERJECTION

> *My Father, the Lifter of my head, I pray and ask that you grant me an encounter of Your Touch this hour that will delete my name from the register of sorrow, limitation and hopelessness, in Jesus' name! I declare that I move from confusion to divine directions in perfection, from trouble to triumph, and from failure to the favored, in Jesus' name, Amen!*

Chapter 8

Experience Supernatural Upgrade

When speaking of supernatural upgrade, it presupposes that there are higher realms or levels for us as unique, peculiar or distinct sons of the MOST-HIGH God. And we need to key into these higher realms in order to move from RUINS to RULES. We need to know and exercise ourselves in these realms in order **to** experience a shift from where we are to where we ought to be. An average Christian can remain at the gate with thanksgiving but a man who wants a supernatural upgrade does not settle at the gate, he makes effort for an unusual praise to enter the courts.

> *"Enter into his gates with thanksgiving, and into his courts with praise..."* **Psalm 100: 4 (KJV).**

The true and peculiar sons of God do not settle for the least, they press higher for the best, pressing into the realms of abundance by walking in the principles of God. Our steadfastness in the principles of God is what opens up the doors of unusual improvement, lifting, transformation, breakthrough, and deliverance in our individual lives and careers. A committed application of the principles of God in our everyday life, gives us the privilege to experience abundance in our finances, businesses and relationships.

> *"For thou, Lord, hast made me glad through thy work: I will triumph in the works of thy hands"* **Psalm 92: 4 (KJV)**.

Following the PRINICIPLES of God would make you a PRINICIPAL to any PRINCIPALITY – Amen!

Dealing with God or operating in the supernatural is all about PRINCIPLES. I want us to examine concisely 12 major applicable principles required in experiencing supernatural upgrade:

1. LIVING A LIFE OF HOLINESS

The place of Holiness is ultimate. Holiness is necessarily the first fundamental decision and choice if we must commit to the integrity of God for the release of the supernatural over the affairs of our lives for a desired intervention and enduring solution!

Exodus 19: 9-11 (KJV).

9. And the Lord said unto Moses, Lo, I come unto thee in a thick cloud, that the people may hear when I speak with thee, and believe thee for ever. And Moses told the words of the people unto the Lord.

10. And the Lord said unto Moses, Go unto the people, and sanctify them to day and to morrow, and let them wash their clothes,

11. And be ready against the third day: for the third day the Lord will come down in the sight of all the people upon mount Sinai.

Leviticus 11: 44-45 (KJV).

44. For I am the Lord your God: ye shall therefore sanctify yourselves, and ye shall be holy; for I am holy: neither shall ye defile yourselves with any manner of creeping thing that creepeth upon the earth.

45. For I am the Lord that bringeth you up out of the land of Egypt, to be your God: ye shall therefore be holy, for I am holy.

> "But as he which hath called you is holy, so be ye holy in all manner of conversation" 1 Peter 1: 15 (KJV).

God is Holy and a Christian who desires His Glory and supernatural touch or upgrade ought to remain holy for God is Holy. When God wanted

His people to behold His glory so that they could believe in Him, trust in Him, and be transformed, He required that they be first sanctified because He cannot behold sin and iniquity. This was an expressive act of holiness which the Holy God wanted the people of Israel to acknowledge. He required them to set themselves apart from all uncleanness, and to present themselves holy before Him. Our Father doesn't lower His standard for any man. This same standard He requires of us today. As He is Holy therefore whosoever that comes to Him must be holy.

We read Jesus' words:

> "Now ye are clean through the word which I have spoken unto you" **John 15: 3 (KJV)**.

The implication of this is that we cannot be sanctified by our own works but by the word of the Lord. As we dwell in the word of God daily, His righteousness in us becomes a visible reality – whatsoever we ask according to His word, **we shall have it**. It is also imperative to note here that it is God who furnishes us with grace and perfects us in His holiness.

Paul tells us:

> *"Now unto him that is able to do exceeding abundantly above all that we ask or think, according to the power that worketh in us"* **Ephesians 3: 20 (KJV).**

Our ability to live in the level of over and above or exceeding abundance is contingent on His power that is at work within us. It is by the working of His power in us that we are able to subdue sinful appetites, and resist worldly lust, and become all He wants us to be **for Him**.

Jesus tells us:

> *"If ye abide in me, and my words abide in you, ye shall ask what ye will, and it shall be done unto you"* **John 15: 7 (KJV).**

He encourages us to make our demands of Him with faith and confidence to receive, as long as we abide in Him, and His words abide in us. He also confirms here that we receive all we ask of Him because we keep His precepts and do things pleasing before Him.

> *"And whatsoever we ask, we receive of him, because we keep his commandments, and do those things that are pleasing in his sight"* **1John 3: 22 (KJV).**

Therefore, when we live a holy life by practicing and agreeing with the word of Christ, we are bound to witness supernatural upgrade in all we do. Daniel and his Jewish brothers had great supernatural encounter when God had intervened in their case because they were found upright before the Lord and before the King, Daniel 6: 18-24.

PRAYER LINE!

Father, I declare that I cannot help myself. Help me to live out the holiness that Christ already wrought in my spirit. That Your word will daily sanctify my life... That my life be pleasing to you. I declare my victory over the lust of this world, and the cravings of the flesh. Amen!

2. A TIRELESS COMMITMENT TO SOUL WINNING

One of the greatest secrets of experiencing a supernatural upgrade is soul winning. This is an act that will always draw heaven's attention in our favor. This explains why our Lord Jesus gave it as a command to us His church – the great commission. In Jesus's words;

"... Go ye into all the world, and preach the gospel to every creature" **Mark 16: 15 (KJV).**

Matt 28: 18-20 (KJV).

18. *And Jesus came and spake unto them, saying, All power is given unto me in heaven and in earth.*

19. *Go ye therefore, and teach all nations, baptizing them in the name of the Father, and of the Son, and of the Holy Ghost:*

20. *Teaching them to observe all things whatsoever I have commanded you: and, lo, I am with you alway, even unto the end of the world. Amen.*

> *"The fruit of the righteous is a tree of life; and he that winneth souls is wise"* **Proverbs 11: 30 (KJV).**

The bible has been very clear on the subject of soul-winning.

> *"How beautiful upon the mountains are the feet of him that bringeth good tidings, that publisheth peace; that bringeth good tidings of good, that publisheth salvation; that saith unto Zion, Thy God reigneth!"* **Isaiah 52: 7 (KJV).**

As children of God who have been saved from destruction, congratulations! Now the great commission awaits you and I, as a ladder that would usher us into the supernatural abundance we desire.

Also, kindly consider this:

> *"Let him know, that he which converteth the sinner from the error of his way shall save a soul from death, and shall hide a multitude of sins"* **James 5:20 (KJV).**

Assuming a situation where one has been saved and delivered from the bondage of the prostituting spirit. Apart from knowing the love of God and receiving the life of God, the reason God saved the prostitute, amongst many other reasons, is that through her, many prostitutes may also come to the saving grace of Christ and know the love of God.

As you read this book today, think about that secret sin from which you were saved, many are still trapped in same sin till today, but God is looking to use you as His instrument for their deliverance. Be challenged and reach out to those souls today. The act of soul winning is like a key that unlocks the gate of heaven for you. Stop the procrastinating – make soul winning your daily habit.

Paul speaks of the constraints he puts on himself in other to ensure that he wins many to the Kingdom of Christ.

> *"For though I be free from all men, yet have I made myself servant unto all, that I might gain the more"* **1Cor 9: 19 (KJV).**

Committing to daily soul-winning will most certainly require our willingness to make sacrifices.

> *"He that hath an ear, let him hear what the Spirit saith unto the churches; To him that overcometh will I give to eat of the tree of life, which is in the midst of the paradise of God"* **Revelation 2:7 (KJV).**

PRAYER LINE!

Father, put in my heart a passion for the lost. Set me on fire for lost souls. Put in me a love and hunger for souls. May soulwinning be my daily passion. Amen!

3. WALKING IN ABSOLUTE OBEDIENCE

One can provoke a supernatural upgrade through obedience to the word, and instruction from God. Obedience to the instructions of God would determine how much of glory will be evidently manifested in the life of God's children, and the level of conquest they will see in their pursuits and endeavors.

We see that Paul the apostle was obedient to his calling, and all through his journeys he remained faithful to the commission, and at the end, he reached the target set for him by God. He accomplished the will of God for his life. All the apostles were obedient to the instructions from the Lord and as a result, mighty miracles, signs, and wonders were powerfully demonstrated in their ministries and callings.

Abraham was promptly obedient to the word of the Lord in all his deeds and it was accounted to him for righteousness, and consequently, he received the supernatural enlargement. The Lord God said to Abraham;

> "...Surely blessing I will bless thee, and multiplying I will multiply thee" **Hebrew 6: 14 (KJV)**.

Because God rewards obedience, when we obey Him, He is obligated in a sense to expose us to a supernatural upgrade. In the Book of Revelation Jesus says to us:

> "I know thy works: behold, I have set before thee an open door, and no man can shut it: for thou hast a little strength, and hast kept my word, and hast not denied my name" **Revelation 3: 8 (KJV)**.

See also the lives of these men of God: Noah, Joseph, Job, Elijah, Daniel and many others in the bible whose lives are a cloud of evidence to us. In spite of the affliction they suffered, they continued with the Lord in strict obedience to the word of God. Their lives are models to every believer of the gospel today. By their walk with God, and their obedience to His word, we are certain that we are destined for a supernatural experience if we do not rebel but remain obedient to God's revealed word. We have a guarantee that if we give our hearts to the service of the Lord, and heed the word of God, doors to supernatural upgrades remain open to us.

king Saul could not operate from this supernatural realm because he was not obedient to the commission.

1Samuel 15: 22-23 (KJV).

22. *And Samuel said, Hath the Lord as great delight in burnt offerings and sacrifices, as in obeying the voice of the Lord? Behold, to obey is better than sacrifice, and to hearken than the fat of rams.*

23. *For rebellion is as the sin of witchcraft, and stubbornness is as iniquity and idolatry. Because thou hast rejected the word of the Lord, he hath also rejected thee from being king.*

From the prophetic pronouncement on Saul, we see that those who reject the word of God are themselves rejected by God's supernatural providence. See again: *"...Because thou hast rejected the word of the Lord, he hath also rejected thee from being king."*

Let us also consider these scriptures:

"But take diligent heed to do the commandment and the law, which Moses the servant of the Lord charged you, to love the Lord your God, and to walk in all his ways, and to keep his commandments, and to cleave unto him, and to serve him with all your heart and with all your soul" **Joshua 22: 5 (KJV)**.

"Not every one that saith unto me, Lord, Lord, shall enter into the kingdom of heaven; but he that doeth the will of my Father which is in heaven" **Matthew 7: 21 (KJV)**.

"Then Peter and the other apostles answered and said, We ought to obey God rather than men" **Acts 5: 29 (KJV)**.

"By faith Noah, being warned of God of things not seen as yet, moved with fear, prepared an ark to the saving of his house; by the which he condemned the world, and became heir of the righteousness which is by faith" **Hebrew 11: 7 (KJV)**.

Now, in your secret places, are you still walking in obedience? Can God boldly say that you are truly His? What about obedience to studying the word of

God, obedience to speaking nothing but the truth to the shame of Satan? Can your friends and other people around you testify that you are a true child of God? Is your claim to God's obedience plainly demonstrated by the fruits you bear? Remember what the Lord God says:

> *"I the Lord search the heart, I try the reins, even to give every man according to his ways, and according to the fruit of his doings"* **Jeremiah 17: 10 (KJV).**

PRAYER LINE!

Father, I repent of the sin of procrastination. I have not heeded your instructions in total obedience. By Your grace, I declare that henceforth, I will walk in obedience to every instruction of yours. Amen!

4. PREVAILING AT THE ALTAR OF PRAYERS

When prayer becomes our life-style, winning becomes our lot before the issues of life!

> *"... The effectual fervent prayer of a righteous man availeth much"* **James 5:16 (KJV).**

We can be greatly blessed with such level of exposure to the realms of supernatural rewards when we sincerely and diligently seek God in prayers about our needs and needs of others. The bible refers to a number of instances where our Lord Jesus promises that we will receive our requests in prayers only if we believe when we pray.

Matt 18: 19-20 (KJV).

19. *Again I say unto you, That if two of you shall agree on earth as touching any thing that they shall ask, it shall be done for them of my Father which is in heaven.*

20. *For where two or three are gathered together in my name, there am I in the midst of them.*

"And all things, whatsoever ye shall ask in prayer, believing, ye shall receive" **Matthew 21: 22 (KJV)**.

"Therefore I say unto you, What things soever ye desire, when ye pray, believe that ye receive them, and ye shall have them" **Mark 11: 24 (KJV)**.

John 14: 13-14 (KJV).

13. *And whatsoever ye shall ask in my name, that will I do, that the Father may be glorified in the Son*

14. *If ye shall ask any thing in my name, I will do it.*

> *"And I say unto you, Ask, and it shall be given you; seek, and ye shall find; knock, and it shall be opened unto you"* **Luke 11: 9 (KJV)**.

The scriptural verses below also **indicates** that the prayer of the righteous can even save a sinner and cover a multitude of sins.

> *"And the prayer of faith shall save the sick, and the Lord shall raise him up; and if he have committed sins, they shall be forgiven him"* **James 5: 15 (KJV)**.

> *"Praying always with all prayer and supplication in the Spirit, and watching thereunto with all perseverance and supplication for all saints"* **Ephesians 6: 18 (KJV)**.

We pray because our Lord and Savior, our Kingdom role model started with prayers, and not just for Himself but for us as well at Gethsemane. **The Lord prayed so that the mission given Him should be accomplished.**

> *"Then cometh Jesus with them unto a place called Gethsemane, and saith unto the disciples, Sit ye here, while I go and pray yonder"* **Matt 26: 36 (KJV)**.

Supernatural intervention was demonstrated by God when Peter was kept in the prison, and fervent prayers were made to God by the church concerning him.

Even today at different locations, prayers are being made and people get their request answered for themselves and for others.

We learn from John's inspiration of the confidence Christians have when praying according to Gods purpose and will, there is undeniable answer especially when we ask without doubting.

1 John 5: 14-15 (KJV).

14. *And this is the confidence that we have in him, that, if we ask any thing according to his will, he heareth us:*

15. *And if we know that he hear us, whatsoever we ask, we know that we have the petitions that we desired of him.*

Our God is faithful to His promises and His words to us. But He wants us to communicate with Him in fellowship, in the spirit of prayer so that He can reveal to us how to plug into these promises.

Jeremiah 29: 11-14 (KJV).

11. *For I know the thoughts that I think toward you, saith the Lord, thoughts of peace, and not of evil, to give you an expected end.*

12. *Then shall ye call upon me, and ye shall go and pray unto me, and I will hearken unto you.*

13. *And ye shall seek me, and find me, when ye shall search for me with all your heart.*

14. *And I will be found of you, saith the Lord: and I will turn away your captivity, and I will gather you from all the nations, and from all the places whither I have driven you, saith the Lord; and I will bring you again into the place whence I caused you to be carried away captive.*

God wants us to pray without ceasing because it gives us constant connection to His frequency. In persistent praying, we learn to hold on to Him in faith, and we learn to tarry in His presence. Thus, Paul tells us to,

> "*...continuing instant in prayer*" **Romans 12: 12 (KJV)**.

Also, we read the words of Paul:

> "*Praying always with all prayer and supplication in the Spirit, and watching thereunto with all perseverance and supplication for all saints*" **Ephesians 6: 18 (KJV)**.

Again, Paul indulges us to,

> "Continue in prayer, and watch in the same with thanksgiving" **Colossians 4: 2 (KJV)**.

And also to,

> "Pray without ceasing" **1 Thessalonians 5: 17 (KJV)**.

And as the end of the age fast approaches, Peters exhorts us to,

> "...sober, and watch unto prayer" **1 Peter 4: 7 (KJV)**.

Paul also calls the church to a sustained intercessory prayer on behalf of all men.

> *"I exhort therefore, that, first of all, supplications, prayers, intercessions, and giving of thanks, be made for all men"* **1 Tim 2: 1 (KJV)**.

The persistent act of prayer undoubtedly provokes supernatural upgrades, and moves the Hand of God for supernatural manifestations.

There was an earthquake when Paul and Silas lifted their voices to God in prayer while in prison, and the foundations of the prison were shaken. This is the supernatural demonstration of the power of God that fervency in prayer can wrought. Through prayers, we are exposed to the greater and hidden things that we have not known. The Spirit of the Lord speaking through Jeremiah calls to God's people;

> *"Call unto me, and I will answer thee, and shew thee great and mighty things, which thou knowest not"* **Jeremiah 33: 3 (KJV).**

God can forgive our sin and heal our land from unfruitfulness **and can also sustain** and help us not to be moved when we cast our burdens on Him through prayers. The Lord says,

> *"If my people, which are called by my name, shall humble themselves, and pray, and seek my face, and turn from their wicked ways; then will I hear from heaven, and will forgive their sin, and will heal their land"* **2Chronicle 7: 14 (KJV).**

PRAYER LINE!

Father, I resume my place in the altar of daily fervent prayer. I receive the spirit of grace and supplication. Today, I take charge of my prayer life again… Holy Spirit set me on fire for intercession again. Amen!

5. BEING DIVINELY EXPOSED TO THE GRACE OF GOD

> *"But by the grace of God I am what I am: and his grace which was bestowed upon me was not in vain; but I laboured more abundantly than they all: yet not I, but the grace of God which was with me"* **1Corinthians 15: 10 (KJV).**

By the Grace of God – God's favor and kindness, was Moses the prophet of the Most-High God able to lead Israelites out of captivity. Though he had complained of what he believed to be his deficiencies; however, when grace came upon him, there came a turnaround in his ability, and entire endeavor including <u>in</u> his ministry. He toured for years, and having gained much education, he was yet unable to come to the experience of any tangible success. But upon his sudden encounter with God at the burning bush, his life never remained the same. And why so? Because he had an encounter with the sources of supernatural upgrade.

This same experience replayed in the life of Paul the apostle. After he had the encounter with the Most-High God at the city of Damascus, grace came upon him. From that moment, he went about manifesting the supernatural power of God. No wonder he was commissioned to testify solemnly of the gospel of the Grace of God.

> *"But none of these things move me, neither count I my life dear unto myself, so that I might finish my course with joy, and the ministry, which I have received of the Lord Jesus, to testify the gospel of the grace of God"* **Acts 20: 24 (KJV).**

It was this grace of God that carried him through all his discipleship work, and sustained him in the course of the tedious demands of ministry. This he very clearly stated as we have already captured above, **1Corinthians 15: 10**. Though he did labor more than other apostles, but he acknowledges that it was all through the work of God's grace. God's grace endowed on him was not a waste because it was effectively real in his life and ministry.

> *"Whereof I was made a minister, according to the gift of the grace of God given unto me by the effectual working of his power"* **Ephesians 3: 7 (KJV).**

Therefore, once a Christian is exposed to the great atmosphere of grace, he becomes a supernatural upgrade carrier. Even in our weakness, infirmities and persecutions, we are bound to live our daily lives manifesting great divine results because our Lord constantly says to us,

> *"...My grace is sufficient for thee: for my strength is made perfect in weakness"* **2Corinthians 12: 9 (KJV).**

And in response to these gracious words of our Lord, we continue to affirm thus,

> "...when I am weak, then am I strong"
> **2Corinthians 12: 10 (KJV).**

Peter the apostle denied the Lord Jesus Christ three times, but this same apostle under the mighty grace of God boldly defended Christ after His ascension, and demanded that he should not be hanged the same way his Lord was hanged. Jesus Christ is the embodiment of God's grace, and so He says to us

> "...for without me ye can do nothing" **John 15: 5 (KJV).**

Indeed, without God's grace we can do nothing.

PRAYER LINE!

Today, by reason of this expository revelation, I declare that I come into a new dimension of grace. In every area of challenge, I declare that I receive grace to excel. From today, may the grace that makes different begin to speak in my life. Amen!

6. INTIMATE RELATIONSHIP AND COMMUNION WITH THE HOLY SPIRIT

There is a difference between UNION and COMMUNION. When we got born again, we got into a union with the Holy Spirit of God, which establishes a relationship. Communion is the fellowship we build with the Spirit on the relationship we already have with Him.

We can experience Supernatural Outpouring of God through an intimate relationship and communion with the Holy Spirit. Seeking an intimate relationship with God would definitely result to supernatural uplift just as the apostolic fathers experienced in their walk with Jesus. Intimacy with God places us in that position where we can trust Him fully and see the **performing** of His unusual supernatural **power.**

Seeking an intimate communion with God means trusting Him enough to expose our all before Him. It means trusting Him enough with our fears, doubts, worries, resentments and all shortcomings. Seeking intimate communion with God means surrendering everything about us to God our Father, and trusting Him with our lives, our futures and destinies. God is faithful. He will not only attend to us when we seek Him, but also release an unusual outpouring of His glory through His Spirit as we position ourselves in an unusual fellowship with Him.

It is in the place of fellowship with Him that we learn to give up **our desires.** It is in the place of intimate communion we learn the obedience walk. In deep fellowship with the God of all creation we draw closer to Him, **drinking from the fountain of life.** Our lives without Jesus has no meaning and direction. Therefore, we must keep cultivating the character of seeking an intimate fellowship with God that we may remain recipients of the secret things of the Lord.

> *"The secret of the Lord is with them that fear him; and he will shew them his covenant"*
> **Psalm 25: 14 (KJV).**

PRAYER LINE!

My Father, here I am… draw me into the depths of Your Spirit. Bring me deeper into Your presence – bring me into deeper waters of Your Spirit. Amen!

7. THROUGH THE RIGHT RELATIONSHIP: SPIRITUAL FATHER AND SON IMPARTATION

The bible is full of several examples of father and son, or mentor and protégé relationship which provoked some supernatural upgrade. Amongst the many disciples of Jesus Christ during His earthly ministry, there was a transition of twelve disciples from the place of discipleship to apostleship. And this transition was effected under the oversight of Jesus Christ, who occupied the role of a spiritual father in their lives. They would not have upgraded into apostleship if they did not have the right relationship with Jesus Christ, their Master and Spiritual Father.

We also take into account the kind of relationship Judas had with Jesus Christ. Judas relationship with his Master was flawed on account of his heart disposition towards his Master. Judas followed after Jesus, but never really submitted his heart to Him. He followed Him, but never believed Him. And this flawed heart disposition to his Master's leadership kept him from moving to the next level in ministry. While others were upgraded to apostleship, Judas was degraded to the grave.

The prophets, Elijah and Elisha are another good example of a father and son relationship which brought about a supernatural upgrade. What distinguished Elisha from the forty sons of the prophets was his right relationship with his spiritual father, Elijah. Elisha had the right disposition towards Elijah. Consequently, Elisha was privileged to have been imparted with the double portion of his master's anointing. This brought about a spontaneous upgrade in his prophetic ministry.

The right relationship between the spiritual father and the spiritual son in things pertaining to the Christian faith can cause an outpouring of supernatural empowerment. This may involve the impartation of supernatural power from one person to another, either by the laying of hand as done by the apostles, or by spoken word as done by the Lord Jesus.

Father-son relationship in ministry requires obedience, humility, integrity and faithfulness on the part of the son as he follows his father. This is **<u>fundamentally</u>** necessary if there must be an unrestricted impartation from father to son. We have a few other examples of father-son relationships in the bible which led to supernatural upgrades.

There was the Moses and Joshua relationship, Eli and Samuel relationship, Paul and Timothy relationship. These sons all made significant impart in their pursuits because they operated in a dimension of supernatural authority – a supernatural authority they commanded **<u>under</u>** the auspices of their fathers. You cannot afford to be a spiritual bastard. Prayerfully locate your father, and dwell faithfully with him.

PRAYER LINE!

Father, lead me to whom I must honor as my spiritual mentor. Bring me to that person who has what it takes to provoke a supernatural upgrade in my life. Teach me to develop the right heart disposition towards my spiritual mentor. Amen!

8. BECOMING A COMMITTED GIVER FOR THE ADVANCEMENT OF THE KINGDOM

From ages to ages, the word of the Lord is eternal and unfailing and those who have held on to His word have witnessed unprecedented supernatural uplift in all spheres of life.

Giving is one of the major ways through which God unleashes his supernatural abundance on His children. Abraham who is the father of all nations, typified and modeled 'faith giving', and also illustrated the enormous blessings of 'faith giving'. When God demanded the sacrifice of his only child Isaac, Abraham did not hesitate because of his level of trust and revelation of God. He had faith in God. Even God Himself gave His only begotten Son for mankind so that man would give glory to His Holy name, and advance His everlasting kingdom.

The Psalmist says,

> *"Give unto the Lord the glory due unto his name: bring an offering, and come into his courts"* **Psalm 96: 8 (KJV)**.

Our Father is a God of principles and order, and what He hated yesterday, He still hates today. And what He liked yesterday, He **yet** likes today, tomorrow, and days following. His words are eternal. His principles are everlasting. The Lord Jesus says;

"give and it shall be given unto you; good measure, pressed down, and shaken together, and running over, shall men give into your bosom. For with the same measure that ye mete withal it shall be measured to you again" **Luke 6: 38 (KJV).**

The importance of giving cannot be overemphasized. God designed the course of the entire universe to operate a give and take pattern. We unlock the doors of greatness by giving. This truth is eternal!

Proverbs 3: 9-10 (KJV).

9. *Honour the Lord with thy substance, and with the firstfruits of all thine increase:*

10. *So shall thy barns be filled with plenty, and thy presses shall burst out with new wine.*

2Corinthians 9: 6-8 (KJV).

6. *But this I say, He which soweth sparingly shall reap also sparingly; and he which soweth bountifully shall reap also bountifully.*

7. *Every man according as he purposeth in his heart, so let him give; not grudgingly, or of necessity: for God loveth a cheerful giver.*

8. *And God is able to make all grace abound toward you; that ye, always having all sufficiency in all things, may abound to every good work:*

PRAYER LINE!

O God, that I may spend, and be spent for the advancement of Your kingdom. As I give in honor of Your name, may dimensions of supernatural manifestations be opened to me. Amen!

9. BY THE MERCIES OF GOD

There is a difference between grace and mercy. While grace is God giving you the goodness you do not deserve, mercy is God taking from you the judgement you deserve. There were times when some of us deserved to die, some of us deserved to be locked up, some of us deserved to fail, some of us deserved the punishment but MERCY SAID NO! It is by His mercy that we are not consumed.

> "Let us therefore come boldly unto the throne of grace, that we may obtain mercy, and find grace to help in time of need"
> **Hebrew 4: 16 (KJV).**

The bible revealed concerning Joseph;

> "But the Lord was with Joseph, and shewed him mercy, and gave him favour in the sight of the keeper of the prison" **Genesis 39: 21 (KJV)**.

So, while Joseph was in incarceration he did not get to be treated with the severity of hostility that was demanding of the allegation levelled against him. It is written that the Lord,

> "...shewed him mercy..."!

Titus 3: 4-5 (KJV).

4. *But after that the kindness and love of God our Saviour toward man appeared,*

5. *Not by works of righteousness which we have done, but according to his mercy he saved us, by the washing of regeneration, and renewing of the Holy Ghost.*

Divine mercy played out her part in the salvation plan for fallen man. Justice demanded that we died being sinful men. But mercy rescued us from divine retribution. Mercy liberated us from the judgement of death we so deserved. However, grace offered us the life of God, the eternal life we <u>so</u> did not deserve.

The Lord speaking to David concerning his son who should succeed him on the throne, said;

> *"But my mercy shall not depart away from him, as I took it from Saul, whom I put away before thee"* **2Samuel 7: 15 (KJV)**.

Apparently, Solomon went against God's law. He is written that

> *"...Solomon loved many strange women..."* **1Kings 11: 1 (KJV)**.

Also, we read concerning Solomon's arrogance:

1Kings 11: 2-6 (KJV)

2. *Of the nations concerning which the Lord said unto the children of Israel, Ye shall not go in to them, neither shall they come in unto you: for surely they will turn away your heart after their gods: Solomon clave unto these in love.*

3. *And he had seven hundred wives, princesses, and three hundred concubines: and his wives turned away his heart.*

4. *For it came to pass, when Solomon was old, that his wives turned away his heart after other gods: and his heart was not perfect with the Lord his God, as was the heart of David his father.*

5. *For Solomon went after Ashtoreth the goddess of the Zidonians, and after Milcom the abomination of the Ammonites.*

6. *And Solomon did evil in the sight of the Lord, and went not fully after the Lord, as did David his father.*

Now, in spite of Solomon's wicked ways, he continued to enjoy his reign as the wealthiest monarch ever, revered by all for his supernatural endowment of wisdom. And why so in spite of his wickedness? Because God already told David concerning Solomon,

"*...my mercy shall not depart away from him...*" **2Samuel 7: 17 (KJV).**

Mercy takes from us the judgement we so deserve.

Mercy is the twin side of judgment. Mercy supersedes judgment in our lives. Mercy is the reason we are still alive today. Mercy is the reason we stand where others have fallen. Mercy is the reason we succeed where others have failed. Mercy is the reason we are what we are today.

The tender mercies of the wicked are cruel, but God's mercy is what we need because no man can survive without God's mercy. His mercy is so strong that it has an eternal enduring capacity. So, we must abide in this mercy as a surety for a consistent supernatural upgrade.

My loving Father, I acknowledge that I miss it so many times. I acknowledge that I have erred and continue to err. I acknowledge that Your mercy speaks for me. Where would I have been if not for Your mercy… Thank You Father. Thank You Jesus!

10. BY DIVINE INTERVENTION – WHEN GOD STEPS IN

"And the Lord visited Sarah as he had said, and the Lord did unto Sarah as he had spoken" **Gen 21: 1 (KJV).**

We see here how Sarah has been barren for over eighty years, but God stepped into her situation and she was supernaturally upgraded into motherhood.

When we anticipate the supernatural intervention of God, then experiencing a supernatural upgrade is inevitable!

When God steps into someone's case, there is bound to be a supernatural upgrade of healings, miracles, blessings, favor, and much more. When God divinely intervened in the affairs of Sarah, she became upgraded to be the mother of **all** nations. Though God had promised her a child **but** there seemed to be no evidence of the promise coming to fulfillment. And when it was the appointed time for God's visitation, the Lord visited Sarah as He had said, and the Lord did unto Sarah as He had spoken and she bore a son at the set time of which God had spoken. Glory!

Daniel was thrown into the lion's den. These were hungry lions that had been starved for some time, but there was a divine intervention by the conquering LION of the Tribe of Judah, who stepped in at the appointed moment, and shut the mouth of the hungry lions. This miraculous intervention brought about a supernatural upgrade for Daniel. He gained maximum respect from the king among other political officers in Babylon, **Daniel 6: 16-24**. If only we can trust God, He is ever ready to step into our situation to shut the mouths of our enemies and accusers.

The three Hebrew men in Babylon experienced a divine intervention when they were thrown into the fiery furnace. God stepped into their midst. And He was in their midst as the fourth man in the fire. The fire couldn't burn them because the CONSUMING FIRE was right there with them, **Daniel 3: 22-25**. God is always ready to take up our case when we rely on Him absolutely regardless of whether we are at the verge of perishing. Irrespective of how threatening the situations may appear, our Father is ever on the rescue. He is ever on time.

When Abraham interceded for Sodom and Gomorrah, for the sake of Lot his nephew and his family, that they be not destroyed altogether for the iniquities of the cities, it was divine intervention that came into demonstration as the angel of God singled out Lot and his family from the inevitable gruesome destruction that sealed the fate of the cities, **Genesis 19: 1-25**.

The bible is full of several different instances of divine intervention that birthed **a** supernatural turn around in the lives of the people who encountered God. Hannah encountered God and God intervene in her case of barrenness, and she as a result experienced a supernatural upgrade into motherhood. She did not just give birth to a son; she gave birth to a mighty prophet! **1Samuel 1: 1-27**.

It was divine intervention that made the ordinary rod in the hand of Moses to part a mighty red sea, **Exodus 14: 21-22**. It was divine intervention that made the ordinary catapult in the hands of David to bring down mighty Goliath, **1Samuel 17: 49-50**. It was divine intervention that made Esther to receive favor before the king and was as a result, supernaturally upgraded from just a maid **into** a queen, **Esther 2: 15-17**. It was divine intervention that made Mordecai to escape death and the evil schemer, Haman became the victim of his own plot, **Esther 7: 1-10**. I could go on and on.

Divine intervention turns us from an object of RIDICULE into a package of MIRACLE.

PRAYER LINE!

Glory to God! My moment for divine intervention is here – Therefore, whatever had refused to work is working already. As God intervenes in my case, I declare that I come under the fullness of open heaven. Amen!

11. BY FAITH

Faith is the SUBSTANCE and EVIDENCE of things in the unseen realm, which is brought into the natural realm as our hope connects with the power of God. The book of Hebrews puts it this way;

> "Now faith is the substance of things hoped for, the evidence of things not seen" **Hebrews 11: 1 (KJV)**.

The lack of faith makes us supernaturally barren and exposes us to fear and doubts about what God wants to achieve through us.

James 1: 6-8 (KJV).

6. *But let him ask in faith, nothing wavering. For he that wavereth is like a wave of the sea driven with the wind and tossed.*

7. *For let not that man think that he shall receive any thing of the Lord.*

8. *A double minded man is unstable in all his ways.*

The absence of faith leaves us unstable, vulnerable and susceptible to the enemy's ploy. The absence of faith leaves us in a very unfavorable position, a position where we cannot receive anything from God's Hands. James warns us concerning the man who ask without faith,

> "...let not that man think that he shall receive any thing of the Lord" **v7**.

Our works of faith must be based on revelation from the word of the Lord. Where the will of God is unknown, faith is unsubstantiated. Thus, we meditate on God's word day and night.

Paul tells us that,

> "...for whatsoever is not of faith is sin" **Rom 14: 23 (KJV)**.

Thus, we understand why Cain's offering was rejected. It was not offered in faith. But his brother, Abel's, was accepted because he offered it in faith, **1Jonh 3: 12**. God expects us to operate in this realm of faith so that we can provoke his supernatural abundance in our lives.

Elijah the prophet operated by faith and caused a change in the order of things in his day when he declared it would not rain for three and half years, and God honored the word of His servant in the land of Israel, **James 5: 17**. Martin Luther's anchor for reformation, when he rose against the Roman papacy in the era of reformation was the doctrinal exhortation to the church on how the justified must live their lives:

"... The just shall live by faith" **Rom 1: 17 (KJV)**.

By faith, Daniel had a nice time with God in the lion's den. By faith, Abraham became the father of many nations. The references in scripture to supernatural empowerment on the platform of faith are enormous. Even today, amongst the people of God, there are diverse faith producing supernatural encounters reported across the globe.

Jesus exhibited supernatural power of faith throughout His ministry. He calmed the storms. The fig tree dried up at His word. He raised the dead. He cast out demons. He healed the sick. He turned water to wine. He multiplied bread and fish. He walked on water. He transfigured in glory. He supplied a net-breaking, boat-sinking multitude of fishes. He did these, and many more by faith.

His apostles continued these manifestation of the supernatural through faith after they had been endowed with the Holy Spirit. They went about demonstrating great supernatural signs as the Lord had promised them. **Jesus promises of supernatural demonstrations.**

Mark 16: 17-18 (KJV).

17. *And these signs shall follow them that believe; In my name shall they cast out devils; they shall speak with new tongues;*

18. *They shall take up serpents; and if they drink any deadly thing, it shall not hurt them; they shall lay hands on the sick, and they shall recover.*

Jesus wishes to see us emulate Him. He had promised that we would do greater works than what He **has** done. He awaits this reality with keen expectation.

Ponder deeply on these words of Jesus to you and me:

> *"…If ye have faith as a grain of mustard seed, ye shall say unto this mountain, Remove hence to yonder place; and it shall remove; and nothing shall be impossible unto you"* **Matt 17: 20 (KJV).**

The emphasis on the subject of faith by our Lord should send the message. Faith is the core of our life in Christ. Without faith, we have nothing. It is very imperative that we know this truth as Christians, and bring this truth to full application in our lives.

Finally, our 'faith-confidence' can only come through hearing the word of God. God told Joshua that His word should not depart from him and he should meditate on it day and night, **Joshua 1: 8**. The many supernatural occurrences that characterized Joshua's ministry was evidently a result of his daily meditation on the word of God. Indeed,

> "...faith cometh by hearing, and hearing by the word of God" **Rom 10: 17 (KJV)**.

The proof of our faith in God is validated by our uncompromising decisions and actions. Faith demands that we take uncompromising steps out of our comfort zones. Like Peter, taking a step of faith out of the boat, and trusting Him.

PRAYER LINE!

Father, I command the spirit of faith to come alive in me. As I meditate on Your word today, let faith be revived in my spirit. The faith needed to fulfill my purpose, I receive it now. Amen!

12. KNOWING, LIVING AND HOLDING GOD BY HIS WORD

We cannot believe and trust God beyond the level of the word of God in us. We cannot know God beyond the level of revelation we have within us. Knowing and understanding the word of God is knowing who the Lord Jesus is. Jesus is the Living word Himself.

The Psalmist says,

> *"Thy word is a lamp unto my feet, and a light unto my path"* **Psalm 119: 105 (KJV)**.

Also,

> *"The entrance of thy words giveth light..."* **Psalm 119: 130 (KJV)**.

Provoking the supernatural move of God does not happen by accident but by taking absolute confidence in the unfailing eternal and unbroken word of God especially when taking decisions in life as a Christian. We should not only know about the letters of the word, but also meditate on them day and night. The word should come alive daily in our spirits.

As Christians, we need to study to know the word for ourselves. This is where divine approval comes in;

as we rightly divide the word of truth, taking precepts upon precepts, line upon line, here a little, and there a little, weaned from the milk, **and drawn from the breast plate of righteousness.**

Consider these references: **2Timothy 2: 15, Isaiah 28: 9-10, Isaiah 59: 17 and Ephesians 6: 14**.

Living the word brings us to the issue of Holiness as God cannot use unholy and dishonorable instruments to bring about His supernatural manifestations, and the needed revival in the land. We must live-out the word that we know. We must walk in the consciousness of the reality of this word in our lives.

God remains the same always. His words are yes and amen, **1Corinthian 1: 20**. It is His eternal words alone that can wash and position us for the supernatural upgrade we need in our lives.

> *"...as Christ also loved the church, and gave himself for it; That he might sanctify and cleanse it with the washing of water by the word"* **Ephesians 5: 25-26 (KJV)**.

We can never be disappointed when we hold God by His word. Our Father exhorts us to hold Him to His word for two reasons in particular. Firstly, God holds His word above His name:

> "...for thou hast magnified thy word above all thy name" **Psalm 138: 2 (KJV)**.

And secondly, because His word compulsorily accomplishes its purpose:

> "So shall my word be that goeth forth out of my mouth: it shall not return unto me void, but it shall accomplish that which I please, and it shall prosper in the thing whereto I sent it" **Isaiah 55: 11 (KJV)**.

PRAYER LINE!

Father, as I hold on to Your word, let Your word accomplish Your purpose for my life. Because Your word never returns to You void, may Your word fulfill its promises for my life. Amen!

PROPHETIC INTERJECTION

Today, by the Blood of Jesus Christ, I negate and neutralize evil trends, bloodlines, demonic tendencies and stigmas of the past circulating my life from year to year, in the name of Jesus! Again, by the unblemished Blood of my Lord Jesus, I declare blessings without blemish also upon the affairs of my life, in Jesus' name, Amen!

Moving from Ruines to Rule

Chapter 9

Joseph - The Man Who Moved From Ruins To Rule! The Chronicle of Joseph

The PENTATEUCH which is accepted as the core of Jewish scripture is divided into five main sections. The first section is the PREHISTORIC story, as recorded in the first eleven chapters of the Book of Genesis.

The second section is the PATRIACHAL story as recorded from Genesis chapter eleven, and all through the remaining chapter. It takes account of the lives of the generation of Israel's ancestors – Abraham, Isaac and Jacob in their given generation. Though the promise was made to Abraham by God, but the founding of the Jewish nation actually began with Jacob when God renamed him ISRAEL.

The third section is the SLAVERY story and the EXODUS of the Jewish people from Egypt as recorded in the book of Exodus.

The fourth section is the WILDERNESS experience, the giving of the Torah, and the journey to the Promised Land. The fifth section as recorded in Deuteronomy, the fifth book of the Pentateuch, gives an encapsulation and a review of the Jewish wilderness experience and the Jewish laws.

There is a historic link between the PATRIACHAL story and the SLAVERY story. This link is found in the story of Joseph.

PRAYER LINE!

My Father, I desire an understanding of Your written word. Open my heart to the knowledge and understanding of Your revealed will. May the express revelation of Your word make manifest Your glory in my life, Amen!

THE DREAM BOY

The story of Joseph begins in Genesis thirty-seven, and in my opinion, I would like to say that apart from Jesus, Joseph is arguably the greatest example of integrity and character in the entire Bible, in spite of the fact that he was neither a prophet, an apostle **nor** a pastor. There is no better reference to a life lived with such unrelenting commitment to righteousness, dignity, integrity and uprightness than the 'righteous steps' and 'God reverencing' choices of

Joseph, demonstrated from a very tender age, even at such a point in his life when it seemed there was nothing at stake.

As a child he cultivated an excellent spirit and positive attitude that esteemed him above others. Even before his father Jacob, we see that his commitment to dignity gave him a special place in the heart of his father. His resolve to live differently from the rest opened the door for his father's special affection, gifts and rewards. Truly the footstep of Joseph is a path worth following. His discipline is well worthy of emulation. His story is very **inciting,** full of wisdom and **motivation.** I believe every Christian needs to study his story over and over again.

Joseph's story began with his dream and ended with his fulfillment. First a dream, and then a fulfillment. Dear one, we need to understand that it is not enough to dream, it must become a reality as we go through process. The reality of a dream is better than the dream itself. So, if you are still sleeping, you need to wake up towards the fulfillment of your dream because the beauty of a dream is not in how well or beautiful the pictures are, but in its coming to pass against all odds. Dreams are not limited by age, at the age of seventeen, Joseph knew the dreams he was having were from the Lord and that they revealed God's purpose and plans for his life.

Genesis 37: 5-7 (KJV).

5. *And Joseph dreamed a dream, and he told it his brethren: and they hated him yet the more.*

6. *And he said unto them, Hear, I pray you, this dream which I have dreamed:*

7. *For, behold, we were binding sheaves in the field, and, lo, my sheaf arose, and also stood upright; and, behold, your sheaves stood round about, and made obeisance to my sheaf.*

It is interesting when you consider what sort of mind such a young teenage boy as Joseph must have had seeing that he had no reservation in sharing his dream with his brothers knowing that they hated and despised him. He knew them to be resentful, envious and jealous of him, not only because they were his step brothers, but also because he had reported them earlier to their father about their unacceptable conducts. Joseph was a young man with an exceptional mind.

Joseph was born to Jacob his father, who is also known as Israel, when he was an old man. Apparently, as it is with many who bear at an old age, **Jacob did prove to love Joseph more than his step brothers.** Joseph was the favorite of his father **Jacob.**

The coat of many colors was a very significant expression of Jacob's love for Joseph. We can reckon that this coat of many colors was Joseph's heir-apparent status, even though he was not the oldest son. What Joseph got from his father was favoritism but what he got from his brothers was **hatred** and resentment.

He was only an innocent, beautiful-minded, brilliant and God-fearing seventeen-year old boy, who had lost his mother to the hands of death. He had only a five-year old brother by the name Benjamin with whom he shared the same mother before she passed. He had ten step-brothers amongst whom he was not popular. A major reason for which he lost popularity amongst his step-brothers is because of the irrational favoritism openly displayed by his father towards him. One of such moments was in the giving of the multi-colored coat. Joseph was more treasured than his brothers. Jacob had great love for Rachel before her death, and it is without any doubt that Jacob's love for Rachel was **generously replicated to Joseph.**

I must say this; favoritism in any family is most definitely not in the best interest of that family. It has been known to brew discords, anger, hatred, antipathy and bitterness. Parents must learn to give the same level of love, attention and encouragement to every child in the family – regardless of their individual strength or weakness. There are no justifiable grounds upon which a child should be loved and cherished above his siblings. It is a **thing** dangerous to sing praises of a child at the **ridicule** of the other. By these acts of imprudence do bitter seeds take root, and spring up into dangerous hatred amidst family ties. Favoritism is dangerous in the family and for the favored child – it is received as love by the favored one but it is outright injustice towards the others.

Favoritism is the progenitor of envy and it was the original reason the brothers of Joseph hated and envied him. And his dreams were not helpful in this regard.

It seemed, it may have been safer for Joseph to restrain himself from speaking concerning his dreams. But this teenage boy made worse the situation concerning his position with his siblings. Not only were his dreams **offensive** to his siblings, but making a show of what God had revealed to him concerning his destiny was even the more **offending** to his brothers. A dream that indicated that his brothers and his father would at some point be subject to his rule definitely did not come across to his brothers in **good fate**.

> *"And he dreamed yet another dream, and told it his brethren, and said, Behold, I have dreamed a dream more; and, behold, the sun and the moon and the eleven stars made obeisance to me"* **Genesis 37: 9 (KJV)**.

DECLARE YOUR DREAM!

But wait a minute! What could be wrong with this Jewish teenager? He just poured salt upon open injury. By announcing the 'season 2' of his prophetic dreams to his resentful and envious brothers he made matters worse for himself. Now, the thing is this, many of us may assume him rather unwise in doing what he did. However, the truth is this: A CLOSED MOUTH IS A CLOSED DESTINY! It really is not enough to believe our dreams, we must DECLARE and PROCLAIM it, and follow after the path of our dreams with unrelenting commitment till they become a reality. Joseph believed what the Lord had spoken, and he immediately announced it to his family – 'God told me that all of you will bow down to me someday!'

PRAYER LINE!

My God and Father, I open my heart to receive Your vision for my life. Give me my own dream – reveal Your purpose for my life. Cause me to know Your will for my life. Lead me along the path of my destiny. May I not stray – may I not falter, in Jesus' name, Amen! Over the years I have heard some preachers count Joseph's narration of his dreams as a terrible mistake on his path. Some have reckoned it to Joseph as an arrogant display. But I believe he was simply excited about hearing from the Lord, and in his excitement, he hastily shared it in great delight and pleasure, not necessarily arrogance. Nevertheless, announcing his dreams only served to pull off his father's rebuke, and fed his step brothers' resentment.

Genesis 37: 5-11 (KJV).

5. And Joseph dreamed a dream, and he told it his brethren: and they hated him yet the more.
6. And he said unto them, Hear, I pray you, this dream which I have dreamed:
7. For, behold, we were binding sheaves in the field, and, lo, my sheaf arose, and also stood upright; and, behold, your sheaves stood round about, and made obeisance to my sheaf.
8. And his brethren said to him, Shalt thou indeed reign over us? or shalt thou indeed have dominion over us? And they hated him yet the more for his dreams, and for his words.
9. And he dreamed yet another dream, and told it his brethren, and said, Behold, I have dreamed a dream more; and, behold, the sun and the moon and the eleven stars made obeisance to me.
10. And he told it to his father, and to his brethren: and his father rebuked him, and said unto him, What is this dream that thou hast dreamed? Shall I and thy mother and thy brethren indeed come to bow down ourselves to thee to the earth?
11. And his brethren envied him; but his father observed the saying.

We really ought to learn from this man Joseph. He heard from God and as a result, he received a vision concerning God's purpose for his life. He received the vision, and though his siblings disbelieved his vision, he was not discouraged; he kept on dreaming and believing in his dream. Those from whom he had hoped to draw encouragement questioned his dream. But Joseph would not be dissuaded. Rather, he pressed on – he believed more.

The peculiarity of a vision is that it is usually delivered to the one of whom the vision is concerned. The recipient of a given vision enjoys exclusive sight to the vision he receives – no one else sees what he sees. This therefore, puts the recipient of the vision at risk of possible mockery, rejection and condemnation. Every claim that cannot be immediately substantiated may remain subject to condemnation.

God is a master communicator and He chooses to speak to men through diverse **ways**. He may not speak to you through a dream like Joseph, but if you are determined to know His purpose for your life, He will most certainly reveal it to you. Once it is revealed, you have got to run with it.

Habakkuk 2: 2-3 (KJV).

2. *And the Lord answered me, and said, Write the vision, and make it plain upon tables, that he may run that readeth it.*

3. *For the vision is yet for an appointed time, but at the end it shall speak, and not lie: though it tarry, wait for it; because it will surely come, it will not tarry.*

UNDERSTANDING YOUR PURPOSE

Knowing God's purpose for our lives is key to experiencing a supernatural upgrade in our lives. In spite of whether or not we find fulfillment in those things we do, in spite of whether or not we are presently satisfied; it remains a thing most important to know God's purpose for our lives – to know His perfect will. *"Wherefore be ye not unwise, but understanding what the will of the Lord is"* **Ephesians 5: 17 (KJV)**. Knowing God's will for us puts us on the right track. Knowing God's will for us equips us with what it takes to make timely decisions. Knowing the will of God helps us define our life's priorities. Because we know what God's will is, our goals and objectives are with precision, our faces are set like a flint. Because we know what the will of God is, we are equipped against life's pitfalls and the devil's snare. Because we know the will of God, and align ourselves with His will, we enjoy His gracious supplies; for where the will of God leads, His grace sustains.

Therefore, we pursue our God-given visions until they become a fulfillment. Joseph's vision ordered him along the right track during very difficult times and when faced with great temptation. His vision kept him, preserved him, and saw him through.

> *"Where there is no vision, the people perish..."* **Proverbs 29:18 (KJV)**.

Your God-given dream or purpose will inspire and motivate you. The visions delivered to you will help order your steps even in times when it seems that the dream is far from being a reality. And do not be surprised if some of your fiercest oppositions come from those closest to you just like we saw concerning Joseph. Still, the truth remains that God who gave the vision will never forsake you. He will always be with you, even when men fail you and forsake you.

> "And the Lord was with Joseph, and he was a prosperous man; and he was in the house of his master the Egyptian" **Genesis 39: 2 (KJV).**

There are two important key phrases I wish for us to see in the above scripture.

"And the Lord was with Joseph..."

And

"...he was a prosperous man..."

AND THE LORD WAS WITH JOSEPH
Taking a look at the phrase,

"And the Lord was with Joseph"

and attempting to harmonize it with everything Joseph went through **becomes** a thing very difficult for the natural mind. One may only quickly take the phrase

"And the Lord was with Joseph"

in an ironical sense seeing that his betrayal, false accusation and incarceration simply did not come across **as one whom the Lord was with**. I mean how could the LORD be with someone and nothing seemed to be working in his favor? How could the LORD be with Joseph, and He did nothing, but simply watched as his brothers plotted his ruin? Where was God when he was maliciously thrown into the dry well, and thereafter sold into slavery? Was God with him when he was framed by Potiphar's wife, and thrown into prison? Did God have him in mind when he was forgotten in the prison by the butler?

Many of us have wrongly believed that the evidence of God's presence in the life of a person is validated by the many 'good things' that are made manifest in the person's life; 'good things' by our own carnal definition, and human standard of course. But it is imperative that we understand that we lack the capacity to judge those things God defines as good. Because of our limited knowledge and understanding of things, because of our short-sightedness, we simply do not have the capacity to judge what God does. How so often have the things we have so wrongly condemned turn out to be God's blessing in our lives? While we may not always understand what God does, we can always trust Him!

We must understand that the presence of the Lord with us does not necessarily mean that our journey will be all rosy and sweet. The fact that a man carries the presence of God does not elude the man from the trials and challenges of life. Also, the fact that we go through hard and difficult moments in our lives does not necessarily imply that the Lord is not with us. *"The LORD was with Joseph"* implied that the Spirit of the LORD was with Joseph, to guide his ways, order his paths, keep and preserve him, strengthen him, empower him, fight for him, demonstrate His goodness in his life, and prove His faithfulness to him. *"The LORD was with Joseph"* – the Spirit of the Lord was upon him, this was why he operated in the gift of dreams and interpretation.

We need to understand this; the fact that things are literally working out favorably for someone does not necessarily confirm that the LORD is with that person. Hard work, diligence, commitment and good planning are factors that naturally bring a positive end to one's fate. And these factors will very naturally predispose one to very favorable conditions, though such a person may not carry the presence of God. Our world gives evidence to this fact. There are many today, who in spite of their profession to atheism have continued to record excellent success in their various fields of endeavor. We do not conclude that a man enjoys divine presence by our assessment of his success. How so wrong we may turn out to be.

And on the other hand, we must also realize that the fact that a man has things difficult for him does not necessarily imply that he does not carry the presence of the Lord. Difficult moments are characteristic of our walk with God, as God uses these moments to teach us and fashion us with the necessary knowledge and experience required to equip us for the successful accomplishment of His assignments for our individual lives. This, my friend, is the reality every child of God must come to terms with. We need to understand that though doing the right thing always ultimately lead to favorable outcome and a good end. But what immediately follows after doing what is right is not always what we hoped to see.

The Lord was with Joseph – but we see what he endured, the hard times he had to go through, the overbearing processes that tried his patience. We see all the hurdles Joseph needed to scale through until the picture of the vision he received from the Lord came to pass. What about our Lord Jesus Christ? God was with Him, He was perfect and without sin, yet He was subjected to the most excruciating death penalty in the history of humanity. But all these He endured for the joy that was set before Him, and now He is forever seated at the Right Hand of the Father.

Following God faithfully may place sacrificial forms of demand on us. Walking with God may see us pass through seasons of trial. Carrying God's presence may have us come through experiences that try our patience. Nonetheless, there is a sure and worthy hope for following the Lord even in the midst of adversities. To this end the bible tells us:

James 1: 2-4 (KJV).

2. *My brethren, count it all joy when ye fall into divers temptations;*
3. *Knowing this, that the trying of your faith worketh patience.*
4. *But let patience have her perfect work, that ye may be perfect and entire, wanting nothing.*

Also, we read:

1Peter 2: 19-21 (KJV)

19. *For this is thankworthy, if a man for conscience toward God endure grief, suffering wrongfully.*

20. *For what glory is it, if, when ye be buffeted for your faults, ye shall take it patiently? but if, when ye do well, and suffer for it, ye take it patiently, this is acceptable with God.*

21. *For even hereunto were ye called: because Christ also suffered for us, leaving us an example, that ye should follow his steps:*

We must realize that following God may not always bring an immediate appeal. Sometimes, trials of different persecutions are the norm. It was a very trying time for our Lord Jesus Christ at Gethsemane, even worse was His ordeal on the rugged cross. There is no genuine success of the spiritual life outside the walls of conflicts, challenges and trials. If your Christian life is always a smooth sail, then that is really great for you my friend. However, those known to be making significant development in their spiritual lives are **same** who bear the scars of life's battles and trials. Though our journey may be rough and tough, we can be well assured that our reward is all worth it. Let us keep enduring for the joy that is set before us!

HE WAS A PROSPEROUS MAN

Considering the second phrase *"he was a prosperous man"*, the context of prosperity here mesmerizes and rubbishes this erroneous indoctrination of what the modern church have believed to be prosperity.

How could Joseph be tagged *"a prosperous man"* at a time in his life when he was serving as a SLAVE? This was not the Joseph adorned in his multi-colored coat, enjoying the preferential privileges of his father's exclusive love. This was Joseph the slave boy who found himself on an auction block in a foreign land, stripped of his family, his rights and freedom, stripped of his clothes, his dignity and pride, and stripped of everything honorable, but his dreams.

Yet we see that this young slave boy was labeled by scripture a PROSPEROUS MAN. This simply shows that the kingdom perspective of prosperity or success is quite different from the way the modern church views it. Money or the things which money can buy does not define true prosperity. True prosperity or success is to know the only true God and to recognize His presence in your life.

Kingdom prosperity is not relegated to wealth entirely, but is an expression of God's favor and power at work in your life to make your life meaningful and purposeful. Joseph was reckoned a prosperous man, not because he was materially wealthy, but because he enjoyed the gracious works of God in his life. While the prosperity of the world is measured in the degree of wealth and material possessions, kingdom prosperity is a measure of the grace of God

made manifest in the life of a man. From a kingdom viewpoint, you are not prosperous because you have lots of money, you are prosperous because divine grace is evidently at work in your life.

PRAYER LINE!

Father, in the name of Jesus Christ, I declare that I am a prosperous man/woman. I declare that because I carry Your presence, I prosper, surmount, I conquer and I emerge victorious. Father, I declare that Your Hand upon my life gives me the victory over all challenges, and sets me on high, Amen!

Joseph was tagged a prosperous man because he was truly prosperous according to kingdom standard, and God was with Him. True prosperity comes from God, not man. Joseph had an impression of true prosperity on the inside of him. An impression that was not disfigured by overbearing circumstance, and this inner impression of true prosperity enabled him hold on to God during the dark hours. Rather than wallowing in self-pity, Joseph made himself relevant by serving others and becoming the instrument with which their own dreams came to pass.

A successful man is someone who has made others successful. This was the testimony of Joseph as he made himself of great service to others. God blessed the works of his hand.

Recognize and acknowledge the fact that God is with you. Acknowledge that you are anointed and highly favored. Serve others with all your heart as unto the Lord. Eliminate murmuring and complaining, and replace them with praise and thankfulness. Know that God will complete what He has begun in your life.

Genesis 39: 2-6(KJV).

2. *And the Lord was with Joseph, and he was a prosperous man; and he was in the house of his master the Egyptian.*

3. *And his master saw that the Lord was with him, and that the Lord made all that he did to prosper in his hand.*

4. *And Joseph found grace in his sight, and he served him: and he made him overseer over his house, and all that he had he put into his hand.*

5. *And it came to pass from the time that he had made him overseer in his house, and over all that he had, that the Lord blessed the Egyptian's house for Joseph's sake; and the blessing of the Lord was upon all that he had in the house, and in the field.*

6. *And he left all that he had in Joseph's hand; and he knew not ought he had, save the bread which he did eat. And Joseph was a goodly person, and well favoured.*

True prosperity is not in gaining material wealth, it is glorifying God through the way we live our lives. Joseph continued to cultivate and pursue a relationship with God – this is true prosperity!

THREE CARDINAL VIRTUES

May we kindly examine three cardinal virtues that activated a supernatural upgrade in the life of Joseph, causing him to move from ruins to rule:

(1) INTEGRITY AND THE FEAR OF GOD

Joseph was a young man of integrity. We reason that from his childhood, up until his teenage days he refused to compromise on his integrity. We know that he demonstrated zero tolerance for unrighteousness. This was why he could not stand his brothers' ill, and he reported them to Jacob, their father.

> *"These are the generations of Jacob. Joseph, being seventeen years old, was feeding the flock with his brethren; and the lad was*

> *with the sons of Bilhah, and with the sons of Zilpah, his father's wives: and Joseph brought unto his father their evil report"*
> **Genesis 37: 2 (KJV).**

Joseph gave his father an account of their bad conducts, with the intention of having his father reprove them. Joseph did not do this with a malicious intent to sow disharmony. But as a faithful son, and as one committed to the wellbeing of his family, seeing that he was not in the place to admonish them himself, he therefore represented their faults to the one who had authority to admonish them. Joseph maintained his integrity. As a slave and as a prisoner, he held on to integrity.

Recognizing the favor and presence of God in his life, Joseph's master, Potiphar, soon appointed him manager over his entire house. Potiphar trusted Joseph completely with everything. However, his wife began to lust after handsome Joseph, and she made advances to have him sleep with her. This must have been very tempting for a slave boy in his position. But we learn that Joseph refused to give in. He vehemently maintained his integrity though it was not rewarded, at least, not in the sense that many may have had immediate expectation of. Rather than earning a reward for his stand on morality and integrity, he got just about the opposite. Potiphar's wife, being humiliated by Joseph's continuous decline at her advances, was angry. She **framed** false accusation against him.

Genesis 39: 19-20 (KJV).

19. *And it came to pass, when his master heard the words of his wife, which she spake unto him, saying, After this manner did thy servant to me; that his wrath was kindled.*

20. *And Joseph's master took him, and put him into the prison, a place where the king's prisoners were bound: and he was there in the prison.*

When Potiphar's wife attempted to seduce Joseph, he fled. Morality was encoded in his conscience. Though no man was present, yet he acknowledged the reverence of the omnipresent God. Joseph understood the need to remain true to himself and to his God. Logically, had he given in to the seductive pressures of Potiphar's wife, he may have stood the chance of the best generosity at the hands of Potiphar's wife, and not the discomforts of an isolated incarceration. However, **though** giving in to the advances of Potiphar's wife may have immediately presented a somewhat favorable gesture for Joseph, but in actual fact, he would have betrayed his God given visions, and thrown his dreams into the prison of wreckage. Giving in to Potiphar's advances would have automatically truncated his destiny, and set his life backwards.

My God and My Father, I submit my heart, my life and my all to You… Prune me of everything that brings compromise to my integrity. Purge me of all that questions my sincerity. Uphold me with Your Hand of righteousness. When my test comes, may I not fail You… in Jesus' name, Amen!

Joseph knew that sinning against God would hinder him from the blessings of the Lord. True faithfulness is being true to who you are in God, even in the most gruesome adversity. This is the true test of integrity. Integrity is what you do and who you are when no one is around. Joseph was able to maintain his integrity because he feared God. For Joseph, it was not about man, it was not about what Potiphar might do to him. He did not consider the wrath of Potiphar his master. His restraints were drawn from the reverence he had for God.

Genesis 39: 7-9 (KJV).

7. *And it came to pass after these things, that his master's wife cast her eyes upon Joseph; and she said, Lie with me.*

8. *But he refused, and said unto his master's wife, Behold, my master wotteth not what is with me in the house, and he hath committed all that he hath to my hand;*

9. *There is none greater in this house than I; neither hath he kept back any thing from me but thee, because thou art his wife: how then can I do this great wickedness, and sin against God?*

When we consider the reaction of Joseph to the advances of Potiphar's wife, two key phrases come to light from the 9th verse:

"this great wickedness" and "sin against God"

The first phrase,

"this great wickedness"

illustrates his loyalty to his master, who had trusted him, and entrusted all he has to his hands. The true essence of moral justice was evident in Joseph's conscience. Upon the weight of his conscience he asked the lusting wife of his master,

"…how then can I do this great wickedness…" v9.

How could he do this to the man who had placed so much trust and confidence in him? How could he betray so depth of confidence placed on him? How could he ever live with himself if he ever betrayed his master's trust? Such act of betrayal would be of great wickedness towards his master, thus he fled.

Disregarding the possible repercussion of declining the advances of his master's wife, he fled.

Choosing to prove himself worthy of his master's trust, he fled. Choosing rather to defend his honor, he fled. Choosing never to betray his commitment to integrity, he fled. Beloved, fleeing may not always be a display of weakness; sometimes, it is the honor of our strength.

The second key phrase,

"sin against God"

illustrates his loyalty to God. Joseph would not give in to a momentary pleasure of sin, and have his soul stained. He feared God. He lived for God. He served God with his life. He honored God with all he did. He gave God the utmost considerations in all affairs of his life, thus his primary contemplation at the face of temptation was how God would feel. God would be disappointed at him. He would anger God. He would lose the presence of God in his life. While Potiphar's wife saw an opportunity for quick pleasure, Joseph saw the lurking of a wicked act of betrayal – **a seductive appeal to truncate his destiny** – a snare to lose the presence of God.

The integrity of Joseph's heart made him see the advances of Potiphar's wife as an act of great wickedness. The fear of God in his heart made him see it as a sin against God. Though Potiphar was his master, he understood that he was more accountable to God. He owed God a greater degree of allegiance than he owed his master. Of course, the mastermind behind his dreams and visions was God, and God alone, not his master. While his master was an instrument integrated into the process of his journey, the architect of his life was God. The fulfillment of his dream was solely dependent on God, not man.

Joseph lived a God-dependent life. Against the clashes of great adversity, his integrity and reverence for God was not shaken. He stood up for what he believed. He held on to his values. He refused to compromise on his moral principles. Against all odds, he stood resilient, he understood that his destiny laid in the Hands of God. He understood that as long as he carried the presence of God, his destiny was secure – his dreams were safe.

(2) TOTAL DEPENDENCE ON GOD

Joseph lived a life of total dependence on God. His absolute reliance on God was demonstrated in his uprightness, mindset and speech.

His life of absolute dependence on God brought about the miraculous turnaround of his life from an incarcerated slave boy to the prime minister of Egypt. The word of the Lord says it, and I have also seen it demonstrated in the lives of many, how that God is always ready to resist the proud, and uplift the humble. The proud are those who choose to trust their own ways. They device their schemes, and take confidence in their own abilities, trusting in their own strength. But the humble are those who look beyond themselves, and confess their dependence on God. The humble are those who refuse to acknowledge themselves; they rather not acknowledge their own strength, wisdom, knowledge, ability and advantages, let alone place their confidence in them.

PRAYER LINE!

Dear Lord, I denounce every spirit of pride and arrogance in my life – I lean totally on Your grace and mercy. Father, teach me to depend on You. I confess that my strength and wisdom is not good enough. By Your strength alone will I prevail – by Your wisdom alone will I overcome. In Jesus' name, Amen!

We see that Joseph never presented himself as one with the ability to interpret dreams. He never took the credit of dream interpretation to himself. He made clear that the interpretation of dreams was of God. He acknowledged his dependence on God who gave him the ability to interpret dreams.

"And they said unto him, We have dreamed a dream, and there is no interpreter of *it. And Joseph said unto them, Do not interpretations belong to God? tell me them, I pray you"* **Genesis 40: 8 (KJV).**

The chief butler and the chief baker of the king of Egypt offended their lord, the king of Egypt, who then had them thrown in prison, same place where Joseph was kept. There in prison, both the chief butler and the baker had a dream. They were grieved because there was none amongst them to tell the meaning of their dreams. There was none to give interpretation. But Joseph demonstrated his trust and dependence on God in his ability to interpret dreams. We read again:

Genesis 40: 5-8 (KJV).

5. *And they dreamed a dream both of them, each man his dream in one night, each man according to the interpretation of his dream, the butler and the baker of the king of Egypt, which were bound in the prison.*

6. *And Joseph came in unto them in the morning, and looked upon them, and, behold, they were sad.*

7. *And he asked Pharaoh's officers that were with him in the ward of his lord's house, saying, Wherefore look ye so sadly to day?*

8. *And they said unto him, We have dreamed a dream, and there is no interpreter of it. And Joseph said unto them, Do not interpretations belong to God? tell me them, I pray you.*

The Lord gave Joseph the interpretation, and both came to pass. The butler kept his job but the baker lost his head. In spite of the miracle of these interpretations, adding to Joseph's plea for an appeal to Pharaoh on his behalf, the butler said nothing of Joseph for two years. Apparently, because Joseph's time was yet to come. And let me quickly add that when your time is yet to come, men will forget you. Until your time has come, your efforts at finding favor with people may continue to meet with unproductive ends. So, it is not strange that the chief **butler** completely forgot Joseph after his restoration to his butlership. Now, most people would have given up, but not Joseph; he knew God's plan would be fulfilled.

At the appointed time for Joseph's manifestation, God gave Pharaoh a dream. This dream troubled the heart of Pharaoh, and even worse, all the magicians of Egypt could not render an interpretation to pharaoh's dream. But in all this, God was at work to take Joseph from rags to riches, from the prison to the palace, and from a place of reproach to a place of glory, in just one inspired moment. And when all the abilities of the magicians of Egypt had failed Pharaoh, the butler was suddenly brought to a remembrance of the young man in prison who once gave an excellent interpretation to dreams that came to pass just as he had interpreted. And the butler quickly said to Pharaoh:

Genesis 41: 9-14 (KJV).

9. *Then spake the chief butler unto Pharaoh, saying, I do remember my faults this day:*
10. *Pharaoh was wroth with his servants, and put me in ward in the captain of the guard's house, both me and the chief baker:*
11. *And we dreamed a dream in one night, I and he; we dreamed each man according to the interpretation of his dream.*
12. *And there was there with us a young man, an Hebrew, servant to the captain of the guard; and we told him, and he interpreted to us our dreams; to each man according to his dream he did interpret.*
13. *And it came to pass, as he interpreted to us, so it was; me he restored unto mine office, and him he hanged.*
14. *Then Pharaoh sent and called Joseph, and they brought him hastily out of the dungeon: and he shaved himself, and changed his raiment, and came in unto Pharaoh.*

Yet again, we see how humbly Joseph placed his reliance on God. We will do well to take this into consideration. There are many today who have continued to fail, making no meaningful progress despite their impressive abilities. Their abilities fail them because they arrogantly take the credit to themselves. Beloved, whatever does not glorify God, God will not honor. When the king learned of Joseph's ability to interpret dreams, he sent for him and asked if he could interpret his dreams. Joseph was ready. And he responded thus:

Genesis 41: 15-16 (KJV)

15. *And Pharaoh said unto Joseph, I have dreamed a dream, and there is none that can interpret it: and I have heard say of thee, that thou canst understand a dream to interpret it.*

16. *And Joseph answered Pharaoh, saying, It is not in me: God shall give Pharaoh an answer of peace.*

Read Joseph again:

> "...It is not in me: God shall give Pharaoh an answer of peace" **v16**.

We see that Joseph never depended on his ability. He refused to take the credit to himself. He was mindful to see that he gave the glory to God, that God took the honor. He did not rely on his ability, but on God who empowered him with such a rare gift. He never ascribed any glory to himself but to God alone who never shares His glory with any man.

All through this wonderful story of Joseph in the Book of Genesis, Joseph's absolute reliance on God remains quite apparent. Joseph never forgot who he was and where he was coming from. Though he found himself in the place of an elevated status as prime minister, yet he held on to his root.

Has God given you a vision? Has God given you a dream? Has He has given you an assignment? If yes, then know this; you cannot walk into the fulfillment of your destiny if you are not exclusively dependent on God who gave you the vision, dream or assignment. Total dependence on the supernatural God, supernaturally positions us for an unprecedented supernatural upgrade in life and in ministry.

(3) A LIFE OF SERVICE

Joseph's life was a life of service. He served in his adversity – he served in his prosperity. He served his father by reporting his brothers about how poorly they managed their father's business. In Joseph's service, as a young teenage boy, he travelled about sixty miles away from home to deliver his father's message to his brothers who were pasturing the flocks in the open fields. Their old father needed to know how his sons fared in the fields. He sent Joseph to them that Joseph may receive a feedback from them.

It must have been a long and lonely journey for anyone, let alone the teenage Joseph. This, as well, confirmed the teenage boy's disposition to serve. In his bid to serve his father's will, he was unrelenting in his pursuit of his brothers in order to ensure he brought word back to his father, Jacob. Some may have as well, returned back home with the excuse that they had exhausted themselves unsuccessfully in their search. But not Joseph; excellent service delivery was his objective.

When his brothers saw him coming from afar, seeing, as I suppose, they had quickly identified him by his coat of multiple colors, they expressed their resentments:

Genesis 37: 18-20 (KJV).

18. *And when they saw him afar off, even before he came near unto them, they conspired against him to slay him.*

19. *And they said one to another, Behold, this dreamer cometh.*

20. *Come now therefore, and let us slay him, and cast him into some pit, and we will say, Some evil beast hath devoured him: and we shall see what will become of his dreams.*

They plotted to kill him, but Judah, seeing a caravan of merchants coming their way, and headed to Egypt, suggested that they sell Joseph to these passing merchants. Joseph was sold to these traders for some Twenty pieces of silver, unknown to Judah that the LION from his tribe would someday be also sold for Thirty pieces of silver.

Joseph continued in service with the merchant men until he was thereafter sold to a highly respected man in Egypt by the name Potiphar. Joseph served his master wholeheartedly, till he was unjustly put in prison. One would think that Joseph would have been quickly discouraged by his unjust imprisonment, but no! Joseph maintained his traditional values. Service was the fabric of his mental faculty. Service was his life!

PRAYER LINE!

My Father, I offer my life in service to Your call. Let my life serve Your purpose – let my life serve Your interest in the life of others. Even in the pressures and challenges of life, may I never lose sight of my call to serve, in Jesus' name, Amen!

Given the painful betrayal by his brethren, Joseph may have withdrawn to his shell. In his hurt and brokenness, he might as well have withheld **his gift and his abilities.** Instead, Joseph applied his gifts to the adding of value to the lives of those he served. He was a blessing to those he served. By Joseph's services, Potiphar prospered. By his services, the prison keeper enjoyed peace, quietness and prosperity. He gave interpretations to the butler's dream, as well as the baker's. He gave interpretation to Pharaoh's dream, and he applied his value oriented skills to the saving of the nation of Egypt in the days of the dearth, and by so doing saved his own family. Joseph served relentlessly.

Joseph did not seek to undermine those who enslaved him. He actually helped them to prosper. We see the effects of Joseph's service in Potiphar's house. We also see the effects of his service in the prison. We see too that both Potiphar and the prison keeper recognized Joseph's ability and acknowledged his presence to be a great blessing. Beloved, If you will not work hard through your adversity, others may never see your true abilities.

Service has a way of putting us on a pedestal of greatness. We see it in the life of Joseph and many great men who have **treaded** the part of service in the history of humanity. **Many want to be great but they do not want to serve, we need to understand that service does not only lead to greatness, service itself is greatness!**

Joseph offered great service in saving the land of Egypt from famine. By his acts of service, he was brought before Pharaoh, and established as the second most prominent man in a land wherein he was a foreigner. By his acts of service, he married into the family of the Egyptian priest, and was thereby elevated into the priestly caste. Brethren, the expedience of service cannot be overemphasized.

▣━ PROPHETIC INTERJECTION

> *In the name of Jesus, I pray and declare today that the stigma that followed me from the womb to make me a proverb, a by-word and a destitute in life crumbles and collapses forever this hour in Jesus name, Amen!*

Chapter 10

The Rough And Bumpy Ride - The Process!

Beloved of the Lord, life is not always what we think it to be. Life is not always the easy and comfortable journey we anticipate. Joseph had his dream. It was God's purpose for his life. It was a revelation of the glory ahead of him. He received this dream with joy and gladness. Pretty much excited about the awesome plan God had for his life, he wasted no time in relating this dream **with** his family. However, little did he know that this glorious destination came with a price. Little did he know that the journey to greatness was one that would greatly try his patience. Though the end was great, but the process would come with much betrayal, hurt and tears. Joseph had quite a rough and bumpy journey; nonetheless, he made it safely to his place of upgrade.

A close examination on the burdensome demands on Joseph will help us understand why God may have allowed some trying times in our lives, what His expectations of us are, and what He hopes to achieve by these times of great patience. Again, let us consider some of the bumps that defined Joseph's journey.

One thing we need to understand is that God will first of all give a vision or a dream to us, before he gives us to that vision or dream. That period in time wherein we are given to the course of our visions or dreams is called process. It is during the period of process that we are made ready and equipped to receive the manifest essence of the visions and dreams given us of the Lord.

Many want to get to the place of their prosperity but they do not want to go through the process. There is no sustainable success without due process in life and in ministry.

The dream was given by God to Joseph. But God started giving Joseph to his dream when his brothers through resentment and envy sold him into slavery. This may sound ironical but **the fulfillment of Joseph's dream actually began at the enforcement of his slavery.**

PRAYER LINE!

Dear Lord, I submit to the process You have laid down for me. I receive grace to persevere along the path of my destiny. May I not be weary – may I not fall. Father, keep my eyes stayed on You. I receive grace Lord, I receive grace, Amen!

Joseph was just seventeen years of age when the caravan merchants bought him, and took him as a slave to Egypt. He was already thirty years of age when he was called from prison to become prime minister of Egypt. The entire period of his humiliation, rejection, dejection and hardship was about thirteen years. The total thirteen years was a period of process for Joseph. And this period of process is divided into four experiences:

- THE PIT EXPERIENCE

- THE PROSPEROUS MERCHANT EXPERIENCE

- THE POTIPHAR'S HOUSE EXPERIENCE

- THE PRISON EXPERIENCE

One important thing to note is that Joseph went through all these experiences unbroken. This is a virtue worthy of emulation. Like Joseph, we need to learn how to remain unbroken in the face of persecution, injustice, cruelty and betrayals. Let us kindly consider a light examination of these experiences that unfolded in the course of Joseph's process.

THE PIT EXPERIENCE - was a very bitter experience. It was a first struck of betrayal. The hurt and grief that must have captured the heart of Joseph should have utterly broken him. He came to inquire of his brethren's wellbeing, but they turned to destroy him. They thought to kill him, and **feign** his death to be an attack by the wild beast. And afterwards, they thought to leave him in the dry pit to die. Their hatred for Joseph was so much that it erased every sense of conscience in their heart. It could only have been a thing wholly overwhelming for Joseph to see his blood brethren display their deep hatred for him.

A lot of confusing and devastating thoughts must have run through his mind, surprised at the heart of his brothers towards him.

Many of us at different times may have had certain **PIT EXPERIENCES** – heart rending betrayal by persons who share the closest bonds with us. Some people may have been thrown into pits of life by some friends. Some businesses and investments have been thrown into the pit by fellow Christian brethren, or by false covetous brethren. Some marriages and family ties have been reduced to the pit with no hope of restoration. These pit experiences in life can be quite disheartening to say the least. But frankly, we really should not allow the PITS of life to determine our PITCH. We must never give up. Putting our trust in God, we must strive to keep our heads up and press on. Just like Joseph did.

PRAYER LINE!

My God and My Father, I declare that every pit experience in my life expires right now. I declare that I am lifted out of the pits of life – I am exalted above the valleys of life, in Jesus' name, Amen!

THE PROSPEROUS MERCHANT EXPERIENCE - was for young Joseph, pretty much like applying salt to the surface of an open injury. Joseph was yet to survive the shock of betrayal, **attempted** murder and abandonment in the pit, and now, he was turned into a priced commodity in the slave market. These men who made a ruin of his life were his blood brethren, people with whom he grew up, with whom he lived. **Joseph became a slave on the auspices of his brother's negotiation.** One can only imagine the thoughts running through his troubled heart as he journeyed with the merchants as a slave to Egypt. Perhaps, mixed feelings and memories of his loving father who he may never see again. Perhaps, a sober reflection on his never again to see 'coat of many colors' which was now replaced with a 'slavery coat.'

"*...Behold, this dreamer cometh*" **Genesis 37: 19 (KJV).**

This was his brothers' address of him before he was sold into slavery. So, 'the dreamer' became 'the slave.' But unknown to them, 'the dreamer' was ultimately destined to be 'the ruler.' The dreams were divine intimations of the boy's destiny, which came to pass, precept upon precept.

When Joseph arrived Egypt in the shackles of slavery, Potiphar saw him, and considering him nothing but a slave, he bought him off the hands of the slave merchants. One can only imagine how disgruntled these transactions must have left him seeing he was a young man of free spirit. How unjustly life had treated him. Firstly, he was taken away from his home, then separated from the love of his father, and Benjamin his kid brother. Then they ripped him of his multi-colored coat. **They made attempt to take his life.** And now, they took away his freedom. What a cruel life, he must have thought to himself.

In view of all the cruelty his brothers subjected him to, Joseph remained a man with a large heart. The kindness of his heart was not marred in any way. He remained open, kind and loving to everyone he dealt with. Nowhere in scripture is it recorded that he became vengeful or treated anyone badly. He remained a kind and compassionate young man. His heart remained sweet and free of bitterness. One of man's greatest fear is being alone. Young Joseph was not only left alone but he was alone in the midst of strangers.

PRAYER LINE!

My Father, by the power in the Blood of Jesus Christ, I declare that my destiny is redeemed from the hands of the slave merchants. The cost of my redemption is fully paid – by the Blood of Jesus, I am free!

THE POTIPHAR'S HOUSE EXPERIENCE - was a slave life experience. This was as well, a most unpleasant experience. The last thing anyone wishes for is to be enslaved in the home of another; where your right is lost, your identity is stolen, and your life is at the hands of another man.

Seeing the way Joseph's experience in Potiphar's house is being taught leaves me wondering. The main emphasis most of the time in these teachings often always bother on how he was the chief servant managing the affairs of his master's house. I presume it is also worthy to call attention to the things he suffered ever before he became the trusted Chief servant, entrusted with everything. He suffered – as a slave, he suffered. A slave in a foreign land is pretty much like an ostracized outcast whose life is at the mercy and pleasure of **his master who bears**

his responsibility. The slave is compelled to hard labor. The slave is subjected to grinding and toiling. The slave is next to the beast of burden. The slave is flogged at will and illtreated for pleasure.

The slave was purchased from the slave market, and resold at the slave market when his value is lost. The slave is no more than a price commodity sold off to the best bargainer. The slave has no plan of his own, no goals, no objectives, no life of his own. The slave is worth nothing to himself. His worth is determined only by the value placed on him by his master. He simply lives at the pleasure of his master. Joseph, as a slave, suffered all of these dehumanization, ever before he gained his master's confidence.

But Joseph was not an ordinary slave. He was not just a slave like all others. He was a slave on a mandate. He was a slave on divine course. He was a slave on assignment. He was a slave who carried the presence of God. As a slave to man, he was in fetters. But as one under divine commission, he was carried in the Hands of God. The presence of God in Joseph's life was tangibly felt. The divine presence enjoyed by Joseph was visible to Potiphar his master.

It is hard to conceive of a condition more discouraging than Joseph's experience. It was a sore test of character to which Joseph was exposed. The treatment he had received from his brothers tended to make him bitter. His slavery circumstances seemed enough to crush his spirit. Some men in such experience of injustice, wrong, treachery, and betrayal would have lost all faith in humanity, becoming sour. There are many people today who are yet to endure a tenth of the sufferings experienced by Joseph, and yet they are embittered against their society and government. They have condemned the world as unfair.

There are very few men who would go through what Joseph went through and still have sanity and integrity intact. Only few will go through such hostility in life and maintain their faithfulness in God. But Joseph was committed to God. Also, he demonstrated such dedication and devotion to service, such that he earned his master's confidence.

So, we find the spirit of Joseph unbroken, under all that was galling and crushing in his circumstances. The lesson here cannot be overemphasized. Let us not fail to get the lesson. The issue of life is to keep the heart focused, clear and positive even in the midst of injustice and wrong done to us. The focus is to keep our spirit bold and unbroken in the midst of all that is hard in life's circumstances and conditions – to be true and right and strong in all moral purpose and acts, however others may act toward us. Our inner world of tranquility and love must not be disfigured by our external world of bitter experiences. We must keep our spirit strong, cheerful and hopeful, though adversities and misfortunes seem to leave us nothing of the fruit of all our labors.

The above is the first lesson from **THE POTIPHAR'S HOUSE EXPERIENCE** of Joseph's slavery. This is the lesson of all Christian life. We should not let the darkness of the outside world gain entrance into our soul. We should seek to be delivered from all unwholesomeness. We should not allow anything to crush us no matter how hard.

The second lesson from **THE POTIPHAR'S HOUSE EXPERIENCE** of Joseph's slavery is the magnanimous temptation by Potiphar's wife, which I have elaborately mentioned earlier, but I wish, at this point, to touch that story again with a different spin.

At this point in Joseph's life, everything seemed to be going smoothly for him. As a slave, he had been elevated to the position of chief servant and his organizational skills had earned him some managerial status in his master's house. He technically had almost everything at his disposal. So, while he yet enjoyed his new profile, then came this alluring temptation, such temptation that would be irresistible for many in Joseph's shoes. This temptation came knocking at the door of his conscience.

The big question is this: where was Mrs. Potiphar all this while? Was she only just noticing Joseph's presence in the house? He had been in the house for some good time now, so why is the temptation coming at this time that he had lived so worthily and worked so faithfully? Why was Potiphar's wife now making her advances at this time that Joseph had his master's fullest confidence?

Why did the spirit of lust move Potiphar's wife at this time to bring down Joseph at a time when he had risen to an honorable place in his master's household? I imagine a lustful woman picturing a young Canaan boy who had grown into a very handsome man with an irresistible physical build, all cleaned up from his old rough and unkept self. Apparently, elevation often meets with confronting temptations.

Also, we can think of Joseph's dream and visions of greatness as again coming into his heart, as he found himself so honored as Potiphar's chief servant. His temptation was, by an intrigue with Potiphar's wife, to rise to yet a higher prominence. The temptation offered the prospective of freedom from slave's chains and the possible rise to a man of rank in the great nation of Egypt. This, and not the appeal to base immoral passion, was the chief element in the temptation that came to Joseph.

There are yet other conditions which made the temptation more tempting. Joseph was away from his father, and all back home who instilled moral values in him. Right there in Egypt, no eye was upon him, moving him to all that was true and noble. Joseph was in a foreign land where the standard of morals was low and where such intrigues were common. He was there all by himself. We do not realize how much we are helped in our virtue by the knowledge that certain lapses would expose us to disgrace, and to the condemnation of society. Joseph had none of these social restraints to help him to be strong and pure. However, he met the temptation on grounds of *pure moral principle*.

Genesis 39: 7-20 (KJV).

7. *And it came to pass after these things, that his master's wife cast her eyes upon Joseph; and she said, Lie with me.*

8. *But he refused, and said unto his master's wife, Behold, my master wotteth not what is with me in the house, and he hath committed all that he hath to my hand;*

9. *There is none greater in this house than I; neither hath he kept back any thing from me but thee, because thou art his wife: how then can I do this great wickedness, and sin against God?*

10. *And it came to pass, as she spake to Joseph day by day, that he hearkened not unto her, to lie by her, or to be with her.*

11. *And it came to pass about this time, that Joseph went into the house to do his business; and there was none of the men of the house there within.*

12. *And she caught him by his garment, saying, Lie with me: and he left his garment in her hand, and fled, and got him out.*

13. *And it came to pass, when she saw that he had left his garment in her hand, and was fled forth,*

14. That she called unto the men of her house, and spake unto them, saying, See, he hath brought in an Hebrew unto us to mock us; he came in unto me to lie with me, and I cried with a loud voice:

15. And it came to pass, when he heard that I lifted up my voice and cried, that he left his garment with me, and fled, and got him out.

16. And she laid up his garment by her, until his lord came home.

17. And she spake unto him according to these words, saying, The Hebrew servant, which thou hast brought unto us, came in unto me to mock me:

18. And it came to pass, as I lifted up my voice and cried, that he left his garment with me, and fled out.

19. And it came to pass, when his master heard the words of his wife, which she spake unto him, saying, After this manner did thy servant to me; that his wrath was kindled.

20. And Joseph's master took him, and put him into the prison, a place where the king's prisoners were bound: and he was there in the prison.

It is not accounted that Joseph made attempt to defend himself of this false accusation. It is probable that he did not defend himself before Potiphar in order not to bring suspicion upon the accusing wife.

He probably thought to spare his master the shame rising from his suspected wife because of the respect and honor he had for his master. He rather preferred to be locked up in prison for false accusation than bring ignominy to his master's honor before the public.

God's vindication is most gratifying and most pleasant. When He vindicates us, He does it to our honor. Just like Joseph did.

Sometimes the cost of following God and persevering along the path of righteousness can be quite costly; sometimes, too costly for us to bear. But most assuring is the fact that such great cost eventually ultimately pays off at the long run. Although, Joseph was punished for taking his stand on righteousness. But if he had done the wrong, he would still have been punished; however, by men, and most importantly by God. Joseph may have probably got a fatal punishment for being caught in the act. Most probably, a beheading, seeing he was a mere slave. It is better to be dishonored by men for taking a stand in righteousness and pleasing God, than to win the world's grandeur by unrighteousness.

Mark 8: 36-37 (KJV).

36. *For what shall it profit a man, if he shall gain the whole world, and lose his own soul?*

37. *Or what shall a man give in exchange for his soul?*

PRAYER LINE!

My God and My Father, by the power of the Holy Spirit, I bring down every spirit of temptation lurking against my life. I resist every lustful solicitation targeting to truncate my destiny, in Jesus' name, Amen!

THE PRISON EXPERIENCE - was the last phase of Joseph's PROCESS into greatness. The prison is a dark place, so you can imagine his thoughts when he found himself shut away in the darkness, and bound with chains. Firstly, he did not do any wrong. Yet he was thrown into the PIT. He still did not do anything wrong. Yet he became a priced slave sold to the PROSPEROUS merchants. Again, he did nothing wrong. Yet he became a slave in POTIPHARS house. He did not do anything wrong. Yet he was thrown into the PRISON. However, he had to do something right to be positioned in the PALACE!

Between his dream and the Palace was his process. There is no true fulfillment without engaging the course of process. Process is actually God's design to build us and prepare us for the greatness that lies ahead of us – the Palace!

No matter how bitter and rough the prison might have been to Joseph, as usual, he soon rose to honor. Even in the prison, God was with him. The noble spirit within him always raised him **above** all the misfortunes and sufferings he encountered. His spirit remained unbroken, the capacity to withstand life's troubles was sustained within him. He was courageous, and hopeful. The confidence with which he approached issues earned him the jailer's confidence.

Genesis 39: 22-23 (KJV)

22. *And the keeper of the prison committed to Joseph's hand all the prisoners that were in the prison; and whatsoever they did there, he was the doer of it.*

23. *The keeper of the prison looked not to any thing that was under his hand; because the Lord was with him, and that which he did, the Lord made it to prosper.*

Joseph was always superior to his predicament. He found himself in prison but he had a spirit which was superior to the prison. Many are in different prisons of life and consequently, they keep wallowing in bitterness and despair. What is your prison? Is it Sin? Is it poverty? Is it a medically incurable affliction? Is it an abusive marriage or relationship? Is it failure or disappointments?

Is it Condemnation? Whatever that PRISON is, God is bringing you out of it straight into your PALACE, in Jesus name.

We need to develop the right attitude and demonstrate the right spirit if we ever found ourselves in the prison of life. Just like Joseph did. Joseph was bound in chains but his heart was not in chains. The shackles did not bind his spirit. He gained the victory over all injustice and all the suffering. Indeed, this course of PROCESS was to him a great time of growth, of discipline, of training and character building. Process equipped him for the palace.

Process has a way of thoroughly preparing us for greatness. Process furnishes us with what it takes to honor God with the dreams and visions we have received of Him. In order that we mess not up the mandate upon reaching the palace of our lives. Process makes us worthy of wearing the crown in the end in all royal splendors.

PRAYER LINE!

My God and Eternal Father, in the mighty name of Jesus Christ, I break down every prison wall keeping me from moving forward in life. As I lift my voice in prayer and praise to You, let the foundation of every prison in my life be shaken, and let the prison doors break open, Amen!

◻── PROPHETIC INTERVENTION

> *Lord, I pray for Your inevitable supernatural intervention in my life that would position me for a supernatural upgrade, in Jesus' name.*
>
> *Lord, step into my case that I may step up in the name of Jesus.*

Chapter

Recongnizing God's Plan - Walking In It!

Sometimes, the reason we make the wrong choices in our journey in life is because we have failed to recognize, understand and walk in God's plan for us. God's plan and purpose for us is His perfect will for our lives.

Joseph knew and understood God's plan for his life. In the course of his process he never lost sight of God's plan for his life. He knew it. He understood it. He believed it. He walked in it. He lived for it. He looked for it. He waited for it. And he manifested it. When eventually his purpose came to light, he spoke confidently to his brothers, same who had sold him off to the slave merchants.

Genesis 45: 4-8 (KJV)

4. *And Joseph said unto his brethren, Come near to me, I pray you. And they came near. And he said, I am Joseph your brother, whom ye sold into Egypt.*

5. *Now therefore be not grieved, nor angry with yourselves, that ye sold me hither: for God did send me before you to preserve life.*

6. *For these two years hath the famine been in the land: and yet there are five years, in the which there shall neither be earing nor harvest.*

7. *And God sent me before you to preserve you a posterity in the earth, and to save your lives by a great deliverance.*

8. *So now it was not you that sent me hither, but God: and he hath made me a father to Pharaoh, and lord of all his house, and a ruler throughout all the land of Egypt.*

It beats my imagination to discover that all along, from the onset, Joseph had an understanding of everything he suffered as being necessary to unfold God's plan for his life. Joseph knew all along that everything he went through was part of God's plan for him. It was necessary that these things played out the way they did in order that he may light upon that platform which afforded him the authority by which he would successfully preserve a generation. Awesome God!

He was thrown into the Pit and it was God's plan! He was sold into slavery and it was God's plan! He spent time in Potiphar's house and it was God's plan! Hey, he was thrown into the prison for a couple of years, and lo, it was still God's plan - God's plan to preserve a generation of people.

God had through the course of process opened up Joseph mind to the big picture. Joseph got the understanding that this was not really about his brother's plan to kill him, or sell him into slavery. It was about God's plan to save them and preserve them who had so done cruelly against him. God was going to use this slave to save his family and a nation.

PRAYER LINE!

Dear Lord, help me to recognize and understand Your purpose for my life. Give me the grace to receive Your will, and to walk in it. May Your vision for my life never be aborted – may my dreams never be abandoned. Amen!

IMAGINE FOR A MINUTE

Imagine for a minute that Joseph, for some reason, had not gone in search of his brothers in the field. Imagine that his brothers did not hate him. Reuben was able to rescue Joseph from his brothers' cruel hands, and prevented them from throwing him into the dry well. Imagine that there were no slavers caravan journey to Egypt. Imagine Joseph had not been sold off to the Egyptian slave merchants.

Imagine also that Potiphar had no interest for a slave boy in his home. Kindly also imagine that Potiphar's wife was able to restrain her lust, and made no solicitation to Joseph. And even if she did make lustful advances on Joseph, imagine she had raised no false alarm against Joseph, but rather let him be. Imagine that Potiphar was kind enough to pardon Joseph, and spared him incarceration. Imagine that the butler and the baker had not offended their lord, and had no reason to be in prison. Imagine also that God had not given them a dream for which Joseph would interpret. Imagine that Pharaoh had not dreamed. Imagine that magicians in Egypt could render an interpretation to Pharaoh's dream. Imagine that the butler had not made mention of Joseph to Pharaoh.

Can you imagine a seven-year severe global famine with no divinely raised and prepared Joseph commissioned and mandated with the task to save the world? Can you imagine a global catastrophe with no remedy? Egypt would have been devastated by starvation, and a large number of people would have died and the savage Hittites would have destroyed those whom the famine had spared. Civilization of which Egypt remains its mother would have been set back because Egypt would have been blotted out.

But the history of the whole world has followed its course just because a Canaan boy was sold into slavery, being pre-orchestrated by God. It was all God's plan – He is a master planner!

> "And God sent me before you to preserve you a posterity in the earth, and to save your lives by a great deliverance" **Genesis 45: 7 (KJV)**.

WHY EGYPT?

Here was Joseph again in the above scripture presenting his brothers with the picture of God's plan for the establishment of the Hebrew nation in the land. The big question is, why Egypt? Why not any other nation apart from Egypt? I believe an integral part of the reason God moved Israel from Canaan by the occasion of famine to Egypt may have been because at that time Canaan was a country of crude people, more like barbarians. The Canaanites were without learning, without a civilized culture, without the arts of craft and sciences. However, Egypt was the seat of the world's highest civilization, reputed for her letters, libraries, education, arts and crafts, and culture.

Therefore, dwelling in Egypt was God's way of exposing them to standard education and civilization. The Hebrew people would gain education. They would become civilized, cultured, skilled and would learn the arts necessary to fit them for self-government and conservers of God's Law. By this exposure, God would use Israel as His message of light in the world. Today, as a result, we cannot estimate what the Hebrew nation has been to the world over the centuries, especially through its laws and its religion. Such a great blessing Israel has been to the world.

PRAYER LINE!

Father Lord, teach me the skills I must learn. Grant me the enablement to acquire the education and training needed to accomplish Your vision for my life. Father, expose me to the experiences needed for the actualization of my destiny. In Jesus' name, Amen!

No matter what we are going through or the challenges presently battling with us, we must not be dismayed. For God very well has it all planned out. Yes, God has a plan. Sometimes, God allows these hard moments in His overall plan for our lives as part of His way of building character in us, making us a formidable fortress.

> *"And we know that all things work together for good to them that love God, to them who are the called according to his purpose"*
> **Romans 8:28 (KJV)**.

Let us remain committed to the plans of God for our individual lives. Let us ask to know His plans for us. Let us ask for an understanding of His plans for us. Let us embrace it. Let us walk in it. Let us live for it. We will most definitely succeed in Jesus name.

THE SUPERNATURALLY UPGRADED

Joseph is lifted to honor. He is supernaturally upgraded. From the prison to the palace in an instant, and his life completely turned around. One access to Pharaoh and he lights upon purpose.

Genesis 41: 39-44 (KJV).

39. *And Pharaoh said unto Joseph, Forasmuch as God hath shewed thee all this, there is none so discreet and wise as thou art:*

40. *Thou shalt be over my house, and according unto thy word shall all my people be ruled: only in the throne will I be greater than thou.*

41. *And Pharaoh said unto Joseph, See, I have set thee over all the land of Egypt.*

42. *And Pharaoh took off his ring from his hand, and put it upon Joseph's hand, and arrayed him in vestures of fine linen, and put a gold chain about his neck;*

43. *And he made him to ride in the second chariot which he had; and they cried before him, Bow the knee: and he made him ruler over all the land of Egypt.*

44. *And Pharaoh said unto Joseph, I am Pharaoh, and without thee shall no man lift up his hand or foot in all the land of Egypt.*

The relationship existing between Pharaoh and Joseph was quite a symbiotic relationship. **Both Joseph and Potiphar benefited mutually from each other.** They both added value to themselves. Here was a dreamer boy all the way from Canaan who had been moving from one experience to another, but was yet to see a manifest interpretation of his dream of many years. On the other hand, was the Pharaoh of Egypt, the most powerful man on earth in his day. He had a dream which needed an interpretation.

So, here comes Joseph with a perfect interpretation to Pharaoh's dream, and in return, Pharaoh himself also interpreted Joseph's dream of many years. By pharaoh's hand, not only did Joseph's father and brothers bow to him, but the whole world bowed to him. This honor was by virtue of the good hand of Pharaoh extended towards Joseph. Yes, Pharaoh gave interpretations to Joseph's dream of many years.

> *"A man's gift maketh room for him, and bringeth him before great men"* **Proverbs 18: 16 (KJV)**.

Joseph was able to interpret Pharaoh's dream by the ministry of the Spirit of God. And Pharaoh, promptly acknowledged the presence of God in Joseph's life. Pharaoh realized that the Spirit of God was upon him.

PROMOTION AT LAST

At last, promotion had indeed come from God. Joseph found himself promoted to a position of power, second only to Pharaoh. It is important to understand that his dream was eventually fulfilled. The temptation to cowardice at the overwhelming demands of the process is always there. The temptation to abandon our dreams and visions due to the weighty demands of the process will always be there. But if we do not give up, we will most assuredly reap.

> *"And let us not be weary in well doing: for in due season we shall reap, if we faint not"*
> **Galatians 6: 9 (KJV).**

PRAYER LINE!

Dear Father, upgrade my life supernaturally. Bring Your honor upon my life. Grant me a supernatural lifting – let divine promotion be my testimony. Great and Mighty God, by the strength of Your Hand launch me to my appointed place of celebration. Amen!

When it was the appointed time for Joseph to be exalted and upgraded, God showed up and gave him a dream that no one could interpret except Joseph. God has a way of making you a problem solver when your time comes. God has His way of calling all attention to you. He has His ways of making you the only solution to a global problem.

Pharaoh had a double dream. It was not an ordinary dream; it was God's way of revealing the future to the king, that he might be a true leader to his people.

Genesis 41: 1-8 (KJV).

1. And it came to pass at the end of two full years, that Pharaoh dreamed: and, behold, he stood by the river.
2. And, behold, there came up out of the river seven well favoured kine and fatfleshed; and they fed in a meadow.
3. And, behold, seven other kine came up after them out of the river, ill favoured and leanfleshed; and stood by the other kine upon the brink of the river.
4. And the ill favoured and leanfleshed kine did eat up the seven well favoured and fat kine. So Pharaoh awoke.
5. And he slept and dreamed the second time: and, behold, seven ears of corn came up upon one stalk, rank and good.
6. And, behold, seven thin ears and blasted with the east wind sprung up after them.

7. *And the seven thin ears devoured the seven rank and full ears. And Pharaoh awoke, and, behold, it was a dream.*
8. *And it came to pass in the morning that his spirit was troubled; and he sent and called for all the magicians of Egypt, and all the wise men thereof: and Pharaoh told them his dream; but there was none that could interpret them unto Pharaoh.*

This dream troubled the king's heart. Immediately, he sent for the highly respected wise men, and the best of Egypt's dream interpreters, with the hope of having an interpretation to his dream. But of all these honorable men of Egypt gathered to Pharaoh, there was none amongst them that could tell the meaning of the dream. They could not solve the problem. But something immediately followed:

Genesis 41: 9-14 (KJV).

9. *Then spake the chief butler unto Pharaoh, saying, I do remember my faults this day:*
10. *Pharaoh was wroth with his servants, and put me in ward in the captain of the guard's house, both me and the chief baker:*
11. *And we dreamed a dream in one night, I and he; we dreamed each man according to the interpretation of his dream.*

12. *And there was there with us a young man, an Hebrew, servant to the captain of the guard; and we told him, and he interpreted to us our dreams; to each man according to his dream he did interpret.*

13. *And it came to pass, as he interpreted to us, so it was; me he restored unto mine office, and him he hanged.*

14. *Then Pharaoh sent and called Joseph, and they brought him hastily out of the dungeon: and he shaved himself, and changed his raiment, and came in unto Pharaoh.*

So, we see that after two years of ingratitude and forgetfulness, the butler suddenly remembers Joseph. When the best of Egypt's counselors failed in their counsel, the butler suddenly remembers an excellent interpreter of dreams who had been a great blessing to him two years ago. The butler acknowledges his fault before Pharaoh and tells him the story of the Hebrew slave in prison, who two years earlier gave an excellent interpretation to his dream, and it did come to pass just as the Hebrew had interpreted.

PRAYER LINE!

Eternal God, this day I declare that my time of remembrance is here – my season to be remembered has come. Father, as Your book of remembrance is opened this hour, I declare that men and women have begun to remember me for my honor, In Jesus' name, Amen!

Moving from Ruines to Rule

Beloved, when God opens your own book of remembrance, your helpers would remember you for good. When your time comes, men will remember you to your honor. When your time comes, the attention of heaven is focused on you, and men are supernaturally drawn to you.

GOD ALONE TAKES THE CREDIT

After the butler had announced Joseph to Pharaoh, he was instantly summoned before the king at the king's command. At this time, Joseph was already thirty years of age. He had spent thirteen years in Egypt as a slave and a prisoner, but his moment of supernatural upgrade had come, and nothing could ever stop it. His time for honor had come. His honor was the crowning of glory for the years of process wherein he endured much suffering. And his glory was the honor bestowed on him effective of his office as the prime minister of Egypt. This was Joseph's hour. And this exactly was the purpose for which he had persevered through the very painful preparation process. This was the cause for which thirteen years of his life has been a preparation. Glory!

Pharaoh told his dreams, but we cannot but appreciate Joseph's response to Pharaoh.

GENESIS 41: 15-16 (KJV)

15. *And Pharaoh said unto Joseph, I have dreamed a dream, and there is none that can interpret it: and I have heard say of thee, that thou canst understand a dream to interpret it.*

16. *And Joseph answered Pharaoh, saying, It is not in me: God shall give Pharaoh an answer of peace.*

Also read Joseph's responses on other translation:

"I cannot do it," Joseph replied to Pharaoh, "but God will give Pharaoh the answer he desires." **(NIV)**

"Joseph answered Pharaoh, It is not in me; God [not I] will give Pharaoh a [favorable] answer of peace." **(AMP)**

"It is beyond my power to do this," Joseph replied. "But God can tell you what it means and set you at ease." **(NLT)**

Moving from Ruines to Rule

HONORING GOD WITH YOUR GIFT

A key lesson from Joseph's response to Pharaoh is that the humility he put forward placed attention on God, not himself. It is important we learn from the manner of Joseph's response. The objective of his response was aimed at humbling himself before God, and also before Pharaoh. In spite of his apparent gift and talents, he took no honor to himself. He gave God all the glory by declaring Him the doer of all good things.

PRAYER LINE!

My Father, I forbid to take the glory that is Yours. May I ever remain humble before You – may my gifts, successes, and my life call attention on You. My Father, I put You forward in all I do, and in all I am. Father, I return all the glory and honor to You alone, Amen!

In the same vein, we are not to let our wisdom or our knowledge get us puffed up. Our gifts and talents must never be allowed to get to our heads. Our special abilities must never lead us to pride. Those gifts that are peculiar to us must never be allowed to rob us of the rewards of humility. All glory must be to God, and God alone. He gave us what we have. He made us what we are. Taking the credit for the honor we receive is not particularly a wise thing to do. We must decrease (it must be less of us) and He must increase (it must be more of Him) in us, through us, with us, by us and for us. Our gifts and abilities must be directed in honor of the Lord. Thus, we see ourselves increasing in Him, as He increases by us.

Joseph rendered an accurate interpretation of Pharaoh's dream. The dream was God's message to Pharaoh. It was a glimpse into the future of Egypt. There would be seven years of abundance in Egypt, and immediately following these years would be another seven years of severe drought. And the seven-year famine would be so sore that it would wholly consume the preceding seven-year of abundance. Now, Joseph did not only give an interpretation to the King's dream, he also went on to render counsel on how exactly to eliminate the threat.

GENESIS 41: 34-39 (KJV).

34. *Let Pharaoh do this, and let him appoint officers over the land, and take up the fifth part of the land of Egypt in the seven plenteous years.*

35. *And let them gather all the food of those good years that come, and lay up corn under the hand of Pharaoh, and let them keep food in the cities.*

36. *And that food shall be for store to the land against the seven years of famine, which shall be in the land of Egypt; that the land perish not through the famine.*

37. *And the thing was good in the eyes of Pharaoh, and in the eyes of all his servants.*

38. *And Pharaoh said unto his servants, Can we find such a one as this is, a man in whom the Spirit of God is?*

39. *And Pharaoh said unto Joseph, Forasmuch as God hath shewed thee all this, there is none so discreet and wise as thou art:*

Immediately, the king appointed Joseph as chief administrator of Egypt. This was an extraordinary position of honor granted by Pharaoh to the person alone who he could trust. Pharaoh took off his signet ring and put it on the finger of Joseph's hand. By this was Joseph officially endowed with royal authority to make laws and abrogate them. Pharaoh arrayed Joseph in vestures of fine royal linen and put a gold chain around his neck as an emblem of his status as an Egyptian prince. Pharaoh made Joseph ride in a chariot next to the monarch's chariot. He rode in a royal procession along the streets. He gave Joseph a new name Zaphenath-paneah, meaning 'bread of life'. This name was in allusion to his acknowledgment of Joseph's mandate, a mandate to save the land from the ruins of famine. Pharaoh also gave to Joseph in marriage a daughter of one of Egypt's priests. This was intended for Joseph's honor as his marriage with a daughter of an Egyptian priest elevated him to the priestly status.

FROM RUINS TO RULE

The story of Joseph was the story of man that was supernaturally upgraded from RUINS to RULE. However, we see that it was necessary that he went through the ruins to get to the rule. The RUINS of the process brought him right to the place of his RULE. All the way from the pit at Dothan to the stairs of Egypt's throne. The pit, the slavery, the false accusation, and the prison were all RUINS for Joseph, but when God stepped in at the appointed time, Joseph stepped up from those RUINS to his RULE. And he RULED over the most powerful nation in the world in his day.

The dreams of the Hebrew boy were long in coming to reality. The ugly experiences were hard and tended by the enemy to crush and destroy the young life. But God was at work all the time ordering the course of events occasioned around his life. What the devil saw as victory was actually his loss. Those thirteen years of Joseph's life seemed wasted. But no, it was not a waste. As a matter of fact, it was the most important time of Joseph's life. It was the foundation and bedrock of the glory that was to come. Had he not known RUINS he would not have known RULE.

Through all the unpleasant experiences God was preparing the man for his RULE. The butler's dream came to pass in just three days but it took thirteen long years for Joseph's dreams to come to pass. Joseph's dream was apparently bigger than him. God needed to grow and develop him through a preparative process so that when the fulfillment of the dream comes, he would fit into it and take full leadership responsibility. In order for Joseph to be in charge, he needed to be charged up by God through process! The tougher the discipline, the more proficient we turn out to be.

ENDURING THE PROCESS

Seeing that Proper Preparation Prevents Poor Performance, we conclude that it is probable that Joseph believed he was being prepared for his life's mission. This was the secret behind his unconquerable spirit, hope and courage in the wearisome experiences of those years. He knew he was under training by God. If we had similar attitude towards life's challenges, we will do well. If we had the same understanding as Joseph had, we would always readily acknowledge that God is at work to make all things turn out for our good at the long run.

If we can accept our challenges and trials as purposeful appointments for us, then we will be able to clearly see God's will for us each unfolding day. Having this simple understanding will free us from the anxiety and frustrations of dealing with challenges from a stand point of insecurity. In spite of whatever we may have to endure, we remain secure in God's Hands, and in His purpose for us.

By this understanding alone can anyone be what God has made him to be, and do what God has called him to do in this world. God has a unique plan for every life but we cannot fulfill that plan if we will not key into it. A fundamental means by which we key into divine purpose is by seeing challenges as purposeful appointments. In other words, rather than give in to the pressures of these challenges, we should learn to see them having purposes. We deal with the challenge with the attitude of learning from it. Rather than fuss, we look out for possible lessons, we stay open for knowledge, and we embrace the wisdom we gain. We make positive the challenge, we apply them as tools by which we are better fashioned. This exactly is God's expectation of us concerning the challenges that come our way. Concerning life's challenges, we may learn to say *'God is teaching me some new lesson, training me for some new duty, bringing out in me some new beauty of character.'*

SECURING THE FUTURE

We need to also learn a lesson from Joseph's method plan for surviving the years of drought predicted by Pharaoh's dream. In everyone's life, there are seasons of plenty and seasons of scarcity. Joseph's wisdom teaches us that the most appropriate time to prepare for the time of scarcity is during the period of plenty. Government of nations came to Egypt, not because they loved the face of Pharaoh, but because of the unique wisdom employed by Joseph who taught that it is better to be proactive than to be reactive in life, in ministry, in business and in governance.

In a sense, our youth stage of life may be likened to our period of plenty, while our old age may come across as a time of scarcity. Life brings great opportunities with it. Such opportunities like quality education, career success, excellent entrepreneurship, exceptional skill acquisition, religious accomplishments and more. But these opportunities do not come to us during the period of our old age. These opportunities logically come to us during our youthful age. If we fail to plan well in our youth age, we will have nothing to show in our old age. Those who enjoy a retirement life are same who made the most of their youth age. Our period of plenty brings us great opportunity to prepare for the unexpected, or perhaps, expected time of scarcity. By youthful arms do we fill our storehouses, that we may find nourishment by our old feeble arms.

In this present life, the bible tells us that we must lay up treasures in heaven for the life to come. In these days of abundance of grace demonstrated upon the auspices of the gracious gospel of Jesus Christ, great opportunity is afforded for the harvest of souls. Also, opportunity is availed us at this time to make the most of our spiritual lives in order to secure our corresponding eternal rewards. While in the light, we must, make the most of the light, that we may be found worthy to escape the darkness that is to come upon this world. Yes, the period of plenty gives us the opportunity to secure ourselves against the time of scarcity.

I know not what you have been going through, where you are coming from or how long you have been in that mess. I do not know exactly how long you have waited for divine intervention. I cannot tell how long you have endured life's ordeals, waiting in anticipation for the manifestation of those dreams you have received of the Lord. But let it be known that God is never too late. God is never beyond schedule. He cannot be restrained from getting to you. He holds the map and the blue print to your destiny. You only need to just to follow Him.

Your supernatural upgrade is not dependent on your natural grade. Your supernatural upgrade is a function of God's agenda for your life. Your supernatural upgrade is piloted upon the bedrock of the processes that God uses to prepare us and equip us for the UPGRADE.

Joseph committed his way into the Hands of the Lord. He went through thirteen years of different processes of downgrades and degrades under the subjection of different men. Indeed, those were difficult years for Joseph. He suffered much until his appointed time came, and he was upgraded by the hand of Pharaoh.

Life had been a journey of RUINS for Joseph until he was transited to the place of RULE. For two years the butler forgot him despite the promises he made to him. Joseph remained in chains and darkness, but God did not forget him. God opened the book of remembrance towards him.

> *"Yet did not the chief butler remember Joseph, but forgat him"* **Genesis 40: 23 (KJV)**.

For two years, Joseph was forgotten in prison. There are a number of forgotten 'Josephs' everywhere, to whom promises were made but not kept. There are a number of 'Josephs' out there suffering from the 'promise and fail' syndrome. They have been assured of a job, a business engagement, some financial assistance, a spot on the recruitment, a recommendation, or some good benefit, they have waited for the fulfilment of promises made. They have longed for the response of all who promised to be of some favor, but all to no avail. They had waited in vain, and their hopes were dashed. They were totally forgotten and left alone in the prison of their challenging circumstance.

But I want to assure you that God has not forgotten you. He has been quite busy with your preparation. Yes, He has been preparing your 'palace' for you – keeping your spot, holding your place. When God is silent, He is working! We should never put our trust or hope in men for they will ever fail us. We are to put our trust and hope in God alone who never fails. He is always right on time – the never late God!

I will kindly have us understand something rather interesting here. Every supernatural upgrade is in alignment and positioning with God's predetermined counsel. The chief butler did not remember Joseph until his talent on dream interpretation was necessitated by a problem that needed solving. This simply means that if Pharaoh's dream had come to him just a few days or weeks after the butler was restored to his butlership, Joseph may not have remained in prison for another two years.

But God's plan required Joseph to remain in isolation for yet another two years. However, when it was time for Joseph to encounter a supernatural upgrade, God gave Pharaoh a dream, a disturbing dream. And also, God took away the understanding of the wise men of Egypt, to the end that interpretation may be rendered by no one else but him for who the occasion was staged. It was his time. It was his stage. It was his place. The spotlight was for him, and no one else. At that point, the community of Egypt's wise men and dream interpreters were rendered useless by God. Beloved, when your set time comes, all contending parties are rendered useless for your sake.

Another thing we may consider is that the butler never had the interest of Joseph at heart. In spite of Joseph's kindness to the butler on the occasion of his dream, the butler totally forgot Joseph. In spite of Joseph's plea to the butler, to appeal to Pharaoh on his behalf, the butler completely forgot about him. But the awesome God, in His infinite wisdom and power, ensured that the butler, even against his wish, remembered Joseph. God commanded the situation in such a way that the butler had absolutely no choice but to make mention of Joseph before Pharaoh. Perhaps, there are some who know of your value and proficiency to deliver, **but have refused to make recommendation of you in your honor**, I see God commanding the situation to make you indispensable.

PRAYER LINE!

Eternal Father, because my set-time has come, I command men and women to begin to mention my name in my favor. Let every mouth that is assigned to speak for me begin to speak, and not hold back. I declare that all competitors for my spotlight are rendered useless for my sake. In Jesus' name, Amen!

Many allow themselves **fall victims to** lots of damages on the course of their journey towards destiny and purpose. They allow damages because they fail to see the bigger picture. They fail to see the true value of the processes they endure in life. They fall short of the understanding of the purpose of God for their lives. God has a procedure and a standard that cannot be compromised for any. Some are quite busy, running from pillar to post, and seeking the face of God concerning things that has already been settled by Him.

Sometimes, we find ourselves running from one prayer house to another, from one pastor to another, making commitments here, and pledges there, all in a bid to bring an end to the challenges in our lives. But sometimes, just sometimes, God hopes to see us endure the process. He is not looking to bring a spontaneous end to the process, He is looking to have us endure the process. But why so? Because He has a purpose for the process.

▣─ PROPHETIC INTERJECTION

> *Lord, bestow upon me the willingness to pray in season and out of season, so that my eyes are flooded with your illuminating light that makes me see the great and mighty things You have destined for me in the place of prayer and fellowship with You, in the name of Jesus Christ.*

Chapter 12

All Round Transformation

After thirteen years of process, a process required for growth and development, Joseph became transformed mentally, morally, physically, and spiritually. Overtime he transformed from the pampered teenage boy to a tough intelligent man with fortitude and unbroken spirit. Joseph transformed to a man who had developed good organizational skills and human relations.

It was about nine years after Joseph became the prime minister in the whole land of Egypt that his brothers came down to Egypt. However, they came not in search of Joseph but in search of food; for the famine was sore. They came for food but met with the man whose divine wisdom made the food available.

REFRAIN FROM PREEMPTING GOD

Imagine Joseph, the second most powerful man in the world, highly elevated by God and highly respected by Pharaoh. Joseph was also highly recognized by the entire people of Egypt. He had the power to kill his brothers. He had the power to throw them all into a pit. He had the power to make them slaves in Egypt. He had the power to incarcerate them permanently. But here they are in the palace standing before him but Joseph did nothing against them because he knows that vengeance is of God. He refused to act in the flesh. He refrained from preempting God. He gave God all the room He needed. He refused from getting in the way of God. Despite the heat and tension of the moment, Joseph did nothing carnal. He stayed focused on God. He took no rash decision. His blood brothers stood before him, same who sold him off to slavery and caused him great suffering that spanned thirteen years, and he still did not act upon his sentiments. He maintained his place, he gave God the room.

PRAYER LINE!

Father, I keep myself from preempting You. I refuse to be an interference to Your glorious work – I refuse to stand in Your way. Dear Lord, have all the room You need. I trust that Your thoughts are good – Your works are perfect.

How many of us, being in Joseph's shoes, in the office of Egypt's prime minister, would have exercised this kind of restraint? A great kingdom lesson illustrated by Joseph's story bothers on the importance of letting God have His way even when we have all requisite power to act on our will. In order to bring about a fulfillment of his dream of many years, Joseph may have simply ordered his brothers to kneel and bow before him. But no, not Joseph. He would not usurp his power in an attempt to help God.

Our character is more tested in the time of Prosperity than in the time of adversity. Neither adversity nor prosperity changed the character of Joseph, rather both times birthed a godly transformation in him!

MAINTAINING HUMILITY IN PROSPERITY

When you are in trouble and your back is against the wall, you know you need help, and are compelled to act cautiously. But the seed of arrogance is not hard to spot in moments of prosperity. Affluence has corrupted more individuals than hardship ever did. Prosperity often causes the arrogant to lose sight of their God-given vision. At other times, men, under the deceptive influence of their prosperous estate, have made attempts to bring their God-given vision to pass through their own design. Even with extreme wealth and power at his disposal, Joseph waited on the Lord and observed as God brought the dream to fulfillment!

> *"And when Joseph came home, they brought him the present which was in their hand into the house, and bowed themselves to him to the earth"* **Genesis 43: 26 (KJV)**.

Apart from the fact that Joseph had been given another name in Egypt, a new name which depicted his new estate, with which he was honored of Pharaoh, Joseph had also been so transformed physically that his brothers could not recognize him anymore. Wealth and power may have its way of bringing physical and mental changes in a man's life. But total transformation is by God alone. This was Joseph's story. A story of true and total transformation. In about the space of two decades Joseph's brothers stood before him, and were unable to recognize him. But he could recognize them. He recognized them because no significant change was made of their lives. As it appears, while Joseph was slaving in Egypt, they were also held in slavery, being imprisoned by impoverishment and the vicissitudes of life.

> *"Be not deceived; God is not mocked: for whatsoever a man soweth, that shall he also reap"* **Galatians 6: 7 (KJV)**. *Life has a way of rewarding and paying us back with the very fruit of our actions in life.*

"Therefore, shall they eat of the fruit of their own way, and be filled with their own devices" **Proverbs 1: 31 (KJV).**

Therefore, be not hoodwinked by anything in life from the certainty that we all shall receive in life whatever we sow! You see, character flaws and professional ineptitude has a way of keeping us behind, abandoned and stranded in life. Our harvests in every area of life is determined by the quality of the seed we have planted. He that is committed to righteousness and excellence will most certainly have the result of righteousness and excellence naturally drawn to him. On the other hand, he that is profane and wicked shall reap also the results of his choices.

PRAYER LINE!

My God and My Lord, let Your hand of transformation come upon my life. Transform me in every aspect of my life. May Your spirit of transformation bring a change in my heart, in what I am, and in who I am. In Jesus' name, Amen!

Apart from the physical transformation that was very evident in the life of Joseph, there was a certain kind of transformation reflecting in his heart. This was the growth and development of character and a loving spirit. Joseph had the opportunity to take revenge and humiliate his brothers the same way they did him; and this may have been logically admitted. But he moved in the spirit of FORGIVENESS and LOVE towards his wicked brothers – this was a great transformation!

Another sign of transformation in Joseph's life as we may observe in his interaction with his brothers is the humility in which he relates with them. This is not the young teenager who flaunted his impressive dream before his brothers. This is a mature and transformed middle aged man, who, having gone through the crucible of leadership, now understands true leadership to be the responsibility to serve the wellbeing of others, and not to have others bow before you.

Though Joseph never demanded his brothers to make obeisance to him, but they actually did bow to him. Joseph's brothers bowed before him, and thus was a prophetic fulfillment of his dream captured.

When Joseph was a boy, he had dreams about himself in the center of things. His dreams were centered on him, his interpretation of his dreams was all focused on him being exalted while others are beneath him. But in the course of process, he became mature. Process taught him that it was no more about him. He learnt that serving others required him to interpret their dream, and not his alone.

JOSEPH BECOMES GOD'S INTERPRETER

For Joseph, it took the refining fire of process to understand that the fulfillment of his own dreams is in interpreting the dreams of others.

Genesis 41: 15-16 (KJV).

15. *And Pharaoh said unto Joseph, I have dreamed a dream, and there is none that can interpret it: and I have heard say of thee, that thou canst understand a dream to interpret it.*

16. *And Joseph answered Pharaoh, saying, It is not in me: God shall give Pharaoh an answer of peace.*

Joseph moved from interpreting his own dreams as a young boy to interpreting the dream of men till he became an interpreter for God. There are two instances recorded in the story of Joseph where he gave interpretations to dreams; one was in the prison and the other one was in the palace.

Joseph's response to the lamentation of the baker and the butler in prison was this:

> *"Do not interpretations belong to God? tell me them, I pray you"* **Genesis 40: 8 (KJV)**.

He was God's interpreter to them, showing them what God's Word for them was. And after that, as Joseph stood before the king in the palace, the king said to him:

> "And Pharaoh said unto Joseph, I have dreamed a dream, and there is none that can interpret it: and I have heard say of thee, that thou canst understand a dream to interpret it" **Genesis 41: 15 (KJV)**.

Joseph's answer to the king reveals a humble spirit. It also demonstrates his great confidence in God; in the presence of the king of Egypt, the highest authority in the world, he gave all the honor and glory to the king of kings, the Almighty God. His answer to Joseph:

> "And Joseph answered Pharaoh, saying, It is not in me: God shall give Pharaoh an answer of peace" **Genesis 41: 16 (KJV)**.

PRAYER LINE!

Faithful Father, I release myself to Your Able Hands. Use me to meet the spiritual need of others. Father, use me as Your solution to their problems – as Your answer to their prayers. Cause me to be a blessing to my generation.

Think what woe and devastation was averted, not for Egypt only, but also for other nations. By Joseph's interpretation was an impending catastrophe averted. Think what it might have cost the world, if no interpreter had been found. Joseph read the divine imprint encoded in the king's dreams. And by this was a great salvation wrought.

THE CALL TO INTERPRETE

Similarly, we are all called to be interpreters to others. just like Joseph, we learn that no one may come in of great relevance without being an interpretation to the dream of others. By interpretation, we become source of illumination to their dark paths. By interpretation, we serve as objects of enlightenment and encouragement. We help people find their lost path. We give them a reason to stay hopeful. Many are carrying great dreams and visions within them, but have nothing to make of it simply because they cannot read them. God is looking to us to give interpretation to someone's vision. God is calling us all to be interpreters, each of us, in our own distinct ways, and in the areas of our mastery.

God whispers His truth to us, and He wants us to interpret these truth in word. He wants us to interpret these truth by acting on them. We may not all publish books, write poems or songs to bless men. But if we dwell by the heart of Jesus Christ, there is not one of us into whose ear he will not whisper some fragment of truth, some *revealing of grace and love.* If we tarry with Him, and dwell in His presence, we will most certainly receive from Him great comfort in sorrow, brilliant light in darkness. If we will stay by His heart, we will know His love, and we will see the glories of heaven, in the midst of this world's care.

By the Holy Spirit, God intimates very closely with us in a personal way. He whispers to each one of us in very unique ways. He speaks to our hearts the secret of love in ways He makes peculiar to us. This now becomes our message. God's peculiar word to you becomes your message to the world. And you are His prophet mandated to foretell it again to the world. May each one of us speak out what God has given us to tell. Perhaps, it might just be a word you have from the Lord – speak it out!

It is the interpretation of what God does that gives meaning to life, and makes a blessing of our walk with God. Our creeds may be good but unless we render a Spirit inspiring interpretation to their articles they remain fruitless in the face of a world desperate for God's touch of grace. Outside the Spirit interpretation of God's gracious demands in this world of sorrow and sin, our orthodoxy will count for little.

PRAYER LINE!

Great and Mighty God, I yield myself to You as the interpreter of Your divine will. Father, endorse me as Your interpreter. By Your Spirit, cause me to interpret Your thoughts, counsels and judgments – cause me to minister interpretation of Your love and mercy to a dark and cold word. In Jesus' name, Amen!

God calls us to be interpreters of His love and grace. We have a call to reach the ends of the world with the love, mercy and grace of God in Christ Jesus. But this may not be achieved by our sermons and bible studies alone, no. We must also interpret the love and grace of God in deeds. We have often heard it said that action speaks louder than words. Our life style and general approach to life ought to interpret God's love and grace to the world. We see that the love of God further interprets itself in kindness and helpfulness. Also, truth interprets itself in honesty, integrity, uprightness and holiness. Joseph was an interpreter for God. We must also rise to that place where we can interpret the mind of God before those in need of grace. If we hope to experience a supernatural upgrade in our lives, then we must interpret.

PROPHETIC INTERJECTION

> *Holy Father, I pray that your ever-cleansing Holy Words forever renews a right spirit within me, making me walk in holiness, and putting me in alignment for an undeniable supernatural upgrade in my life, in Jesus' name.*

CONCLUSION

The personal traits and dispositions of these great men as shown in the reference scriptures of this book are a colossus evidence of a life spent on the platform of Kingdom faith and purpose. Worthy of note are their undying commitment to Humility, Diligence, Dedication, Discipline, Character, Perseverance, Courage, and Teach-ability even in the face of adversity. These were their strengths. It was also their means to kingdom exploits and supernatural turnaround in their individual lives. By these virtues, they went from ordinary to extraordinary. They went from the wilderness to the palace. They went from obscurity to authority. They went from hopelessness to endless hope. And I hope also, being the underlying inspiration for this book, that we all may learn of these bible personalities, and as well, harness these supernatural dimensions that so graciously awaits us all.

THE DOOR IS OPEN!!

Christ Jesus, the Lord and Savior of the world calls out to you today. He died for your sins, that you may live in His righteousness. Receive Jesus Christ, He will receive you in love, and grant you eternal life in Him.

Why continue in bondage when freedom is here? Why dwell in darkness when the light is shining? Why tarry in the world when the Kingdom of God is here? Why die in sin when abundant life is available in Jesus Christ?

Come to Jesus today – receive eternal life – receive your place in God's kingdom. THE DOOR IS OPEN!

Say these words of prayer:

Lord Jesus, I come to You today as a sinner needing forgiveness. I confess You as my Lord and Savior. I believe that You died for my sins. Cleanse me with Your Precious Blood. And grant me the gift of eternal life. Amen!

DISMANTLING THE DEMONIC BARRICADES OF THE ISSUES OF LIFE - Living above the Norm!

In this Book, you will be exposed to the power and grace necessary to prevail over the curses and the afflictions of life.

FROM DESTITUTE TO DESTINY

This book is a message of hope and direction, inspired by God's breath to help those waiting for the stirring of the waters, to know and experience the outpouring of God's Mighty power and miraculous intervention!

REDEEMED & ENTHRONED TO REIGN

This Book brings to your life an awareness and a revolution that will position to reign in life over the hostile challenges and confrontations in this dark world.

A 21 day power point devotional, targeting all possible limitations imposed against your prosperity and well being in Christ Jesus. In this Book, discover the God giving potentials and spiritual authority that are yours in Christ Jesus.

IF THIS THIS BOOK HAS BLESSED AND INSPIRED YOU, WE WILL APPRECIATE A FEEDBACK FROM YOU.

WRITE TO US@

@Peculiar_nation@hotmail.com

Contact or follow us on Facebook:
ISAAC MAXWELL.

PAGE: Licensed Limit Breakers - Peculiar Nation in Christ.

www.ingramcontent.com/pod-product-compliance
Lightning Source LLC
Chambersburg PA
CBHW021938240426
43668CB00036B/162